MW01076449

Praying the Anglican Rosary

Gentle Prayer for Daily Life

William Ingle Gillis

Texano Cymru Books

All original additions to or arrangements of the public domain material contained herein are copyright © 2024 by William Ingle-Gillis and may not be reproduced for commercial use in any form without written permission from the publisher or author, except as permitted by U.S. copyright law. All rights reserved worldwide.

Non-commercial reproduction for worship, prayer groups, and local church publications (such as newsletters or readings sheets) is permitted.

ISBN-13: 978-1-965232-00-2 (paperback edition)

ISBN-13: 978-1-965232-01-9 (ebook edition)

The texts employed in this book are taken from public domain sources, wherever possible.

Scripture quotations, unless otherwise noted, are taken from the World English Bible, Classic or Updated Edition. Both are in the public domain. "World English Bible" is a trademark which identifies only faithful copies of the versions published at *eBible.org*. Passages with amendments to WEB or WEBu texts are clearly marked. In all instances, the following amendments are made to the WEB Classic Edition texts: (a) the Tetragrammaton is rendered as "Lord" or "God", (b) American spellings are rendered in British English, and (c) contractions are rendered as full words. The author makes no representation that any given text, marked or unmarked, qualifies to be labelled "World English Bible".

Some scripture quotations are from the New Revised Standard Version Updated Edition. Copyright © 2021 National Council of Churches of Christ in the United States of America. Used by permission. All rights reserved worldwide.

Most liturgical content is taken from the Episcopal Church, *The Book of Common Prayer* (New York: Church Publishing), 1979, which is in the public domain. Amendments are marked, and American spellings from this source have also been rendered in British English.

One prayer borrows material from the musical work by James Healey Willan, *The Reproaches* (London: Novello & Co.), 1912, public domain. A few others are from well-known public domain hymns.

The following symbols and abbreviations are used throughout to denote sources:

✳ World English Bible
※ American Standard Version
‡ King James Version
NRSV New Revised Standard Version
◊ *The Book of Common Prayer,* 1979
† Text amended by author

For Sally and Eli,
to each of whom I owe a book.
And for Mama.

Contents

About the Anglican Rosary

SOMETHING FAMILIAR,
SOMETHING FRESH,
SOMETHING FOR THE SPIRIT

Something Familiar

Familiar? Well, maybe. Or maybe not. That sort of depends on where you're coming from. It is to be hoped, after all, that this book may be valuable not just to the Anglican community, but to Christians of many traditions … or to those just exploring. All are welcome and invited to "taste and see".

Prayer with beads has not, in truth, created much visible space for itself within the usual range of Anglican spiritual practice (although, to be sure, prayer using the Roman Catholic rosary has been going on gently in Anglo-Catholic circles for a very long time indeed). In fact, the Anglican version of the rosary for which this book and these prayers are designed came about only in the late twentieth century.

However, repetition of prayer and chants is deeply rooted in ancient Christian monastic practice, which made use of pebbles in the earliest days; and, indeed, we can find analogues in most major religious traditions across the world. (Traditions of prayer with beads or knotted rope exist in Buddhism, Hinduism, Islam, Shinto, Baha'i, to name just a few.) It is from this venerable tradition that western Christians ultimately developed the rosary that we find in the Roman Catholic Church and the eastern Churches developed the Orthodox prayer rope — both being centuries old at this point.

The Anglican rosary finds its inspiration in both of these forms, eastern and western, as well as perhaps in the lesser-known Paternoster cord; this background is reflected in the shape, numbers of beads, and practice. In other words, although we also bring our own symbolism to the table — more on this in the following chapter — the Anglican rosary did not just start from scratch; it comes from a patrimony that predates the Church of England as an autonomous entity, but to which Anglicanism has always laid claim and which remains a vital part of our heritage.

Therefore, if, on the one hand, you are used to praying with beads in general, the experience with these specific beads will feel instantly familiar and recognisable. The principle is the same: a repetition of simple prayers and scripture, with the aim of opening ourselves to God's presence and his work in the patterns and in the silences.

On the other hand, if you have no experience with this type of prayer — and many coming from Anglican or Protestant traditions may not — or may well be wary of it — please be assured that the practice is simple and easy to learn, and that it can be shaped to work with a variety of spiritual practices and thought.

Something Fresh

For those who do have some prior experience of prayer with beads, what makes the Anglican rosary distinct is that the prayers are notably flexible. The Catholic rosary is famously associated with the Hail Mary, of course; whereas the Orthodox prayer rope, less familiar to western Christians, is based on repetitions of the Jesus Prayer ("Lord Jesus Christ, Son of God, have mercy upon me, a sinner"). In comparison, the Anglican rosary has no specific set of prayers generally prescribed.

This is not to say that Catholic and Orthodox prayer beads cannot be used just as flexibly. They can. Nor is it to say that the traditional Hail Marys and Jesus Prayers cannot be prayed with an Anglican rosary. Of course they can (and, in fact, the first set of prayers in this book will show you how). However, whereas the former two are associated deeply with particular traditions and prayers, and have been for centuries, the Anglican rosary simply is not. In that sense, flexibility and experimentation with the prayers is built into the ethos, and that is where the freshness comes in.

Anglican tradition in general has always set great store by public common prayer as the root of its spirituality — choral Matins or Evensong, well-orchestrated, perhaps being the most distinctive and characteristic examples. In this respect, whilst there is no single equivalent to the Hail Mary or Jesus Prayer that jumps out as a candidate for the one definitive Anglican rosary prayer, what we do have in the Daily Office (*i.e.,* Morning Prayer, Evening Prayer, and others) is potentially a good starting point: a pattern of prayer well placed to introduce and inform our use of the beads, and to which the beads may bring their own value. The notion is to draw from the richness of our familiar liturgical tradition and character using well-beloved, comforting words from *The Book of Common Prayer* to make space in a different way for seeking a deeper encounter with God.

From there, we can find many jumping off points: we can stick with cherished words ("O, Lord, open thou our lips, and our mouths shall show forth thy praise") or begin to explore the words of scripture that we've heard on Sunday ("For God so loved the world that he sent his only-begotten Son …"), or the Psalms ("The Lord is my shepherd …"), or the famous prayers of the saints ("Make me a channel of your peace"). We can pray along with the Church calendar and seasons, and look to delve deep, over time, into the rhythms of the Christian year. We can offer special prayers on our beads for celebration of the saints or to commemorate the feasts and fasts of the Church. Or we can offer by name our loved ones, living and dead, into the care of God who created them.

The possibilities are endless … but if you don't know where to begin, don't worry: we can pray together. That's what this book is about.

Something for the Spirit

Praying with beads is, ultimately, a form of meditation. When we pray the words in repetition, we are presented with an opportunity to reflect upon or sit with our prayers at a growing depth. This is the core truth behind any rosary or prayer rope that you might have encountered, and this is the truth that creates the depth of personal devotion that you may well have witnessed in traditions that have embraced such prayer over the centuries.

There are other types of meditation and contemplation, of course, which likewise draw on the richness of Christian tradition to create time and space — a haven of stillness and sacredness — in the midst of our busy lives. *Lectio divina*, to take one example, is a practice that invites us to read scripture slowly and deliberately, listening for God's prompting at each word — reading not to study, but rather *to hear* and to comprehend and to feel the divine voice. In a similar manner, imaginative contemplation provides the seeker with a method for placing him- or herself within the stories of scripture and discovering what God is working in him or her, personally, within the very telling of the story.

The Anglican rosary is capable of drawing a little bit on all of these methods (and surely others), depending on the specific set of prayers, to one degree or another. Used with a Hail Mary or a Jesus Prayer, you may find the experience echoes those of the rosaries on which this one is based. Used to pray the Daily Office, you may find the comfort of the familiar prayers grounding you as you contemplate God's presence in the course of your day. Used to pray with scripture, you may find a holy rhythm in the ancient words of the prophets and the Gospels as you listen for God's voice in your heart; or you may find that the words Christ spoke to his disciples, he is now speaking directly to you.

Explaining the background, however, and the types of prayer possible is all well and good; but, in the end, nothing can really break down for the casual reader what mediative prayer is really like. Prayer of this type is simply something that must be done for a little while and encountered before it can really be known. Only then can you see whether this practice is something that fits your spirituality or not. (And, by the way, you need feel no shame if it's not.)

And so this book is designed not to instruct anyone on the principles of prayer nor to analyse a spirituality, but rather to get us praying. After the next chapter, which will take you through how the pattern of rosary prayers actually works, the rest consists simply of prayers to be prayed in daily life.

This book is meant to give both individuals praying alone and groups praying together a wide variety of options for praying: with traditional rosary style prayers, or with characteristically Anglican language, or with the life and cycle of the Church seasons and celebrations, or with themes and special intentions. You are encouraged to explore any and all of them to see what might work for you and thus help you to hear and reflect upon what God might be saying to you.

It is my prayer that God may offer us the possibility of discovering new depths in the prayers every time we pray them. And that, through silences between the prayers, we may find ourselves in enough sacred space to listen for and encounter the still, small voice of God.

How to Pray with Anglican Beads

Some Background

The prayers in this book are laid out for use by either individuals or groups. Group prayer in this style normally involves some form of call-and-response approach, and so these prayers mostly alternate between the prayer leader's lines and the group's (the latter in bold). Solo practitioners can, of course, simply pray straight through.

The Anglican rosary consists of a circular set of beads, grouped into sevens, with divider beads in between, and a tail at one end containing one extra bead and a cross. The shape will be instantly recognisable to anyone who has ever held a Catholic rosary; only the number of beads and groups differs.

In total, there are thirty-three beads, which reminds us of the number of years that Christ dwelled on earth and his age at the crucifixion. These are divided into groups of seven, known as *weeks* (much as the groupings of ten in Catholic rosaries are known as *decades*). Seven is traditionally a holy number, denoting perfection, in scriptural numerology. Dividing the weeks, you'll find four beads — one each at the twelve, three, six, and nine o'clock positions — which are often larger or otherwise set apart from the others. These are the *cruciform beads*, so named after the shape of the cross that they make when the set is laid flat and even. Finally, the tail at the end — or really at the beginning — consists of the thirty-third bead, the *invitatory bead*, named for the inviting and centring intentions that normally underlie the prayer assigned to it, along with a *cross* or a *crucifix* placed just before it to start the prayers with a reminder of Christ.

Praying the Beads

To begin, it is suggested that you find a quiet space, if possible, then take a few moments to be still and breathe, to ask gently for God's Spirit to be present with you, and to centre yourself in readiness for prayer.

Then, after a moment, hold the beads in your hand, and the cross in your fingers, and begin to work your way around the prayers assigned for each part of the rosary — one for the cross, then one for each bead, in the pattern described below.

(1) The Cross: We begin our prayers with the Cross, the symbol of salvation. The opening prayer tends to be strong and familiar and gives a clear signal of our Christian intentions: common prayers might include, for example, the Apostles' Creed or the Our Father.

(2) The Invitatory Bead: As suggested above, this bead marks a moment when we are invited to come further into God's presence. Here we find a prayer meant to mark the tone or set a theme for the session to follow — one that invites us to offer ourselves in depth: it might be, for example, a psalm of praise, or words of hope, or even a prayer of sorrow.

(3) The Cruciform Beads: With the cruciform beads, we begin working towards the repetitions of simple prayers, and making our way around the circle. These beads provide bookends for the weeks; they lead us a little more deeply into the reflection, theme, or story that we are praying. Normally simpler than the Cross and the invitatory prayers, the cruciform beads nonetheless serve as markers that remind us to pause in our repetitions, to listen for God, and not to lose the wider scope of our prayer pattern.

(4) The Weeks: Following each cruciform bead, then, is the set of seven: the weeks. With these beads, we generally pray a phrase, something very short and simple, slowly, in repetition seven times, making deliberate pauses in between each one: for example, "Bless the Lord, O my soul, and let all that is within me bless his holy name". This slow, spaced repetition and the very simplicity of the words help us to inhabit the prayer and find stillness in God's presence.

In this book, the custom will be to conclude each week with the *Gloria Patri* ("Glory be to the Father, and to the Son, and to the Holy Spirit …") to draw together and finish the week at hand and to mark the cycle's transition into the next week … which begins again with the next cruciform bead.

(5) The Dimissory Bead: Finally, after praying all the way round the circle, we return to that first cruciform bead, which now serves gently to conclude our prayers and to bring us back afresh to daily life. Normally, as the name implies, this final prayer of the series carries the sense of dismissal — for example, the *Nunc dimittis:* "Lord, now let your servant depart in peace …". It is often a good idea to spend a little while in silence after prayer — for as long or as short as you like — simply to help you emerge gently from this sacred space that you've created with God and to carry it in some way back into the world.

8

• • •

Having done all that, well done! You've now prayed your first Anglican rosary, and may God bless you on your way.

Core Prayers

Cross

In the name of the Father, and of the Son,
and of the Holy Spirit. **Amen.**

O God, make speed to save us.
O Lord, make haste to help us.
— *Evening Prayer II*◊

Invitatory

Holy God,
Holy and Mighty,
Holy Immortal One,
have mercy upon us.
— *Trisagion*◊

Cruciform

Our Father,
who art in heaven,
hallowed be thy name.
Thy kingdom come;
thy will be done
on earth as it is in heaven.
Give us this day our daily bread,
and forgive us our trespasses
as we forgive those who trespass against us.
And lead us not into temptation,
but deliver us from evil.
For thine is the kingdom,
and the power, and the glory,
for ever and ever. Amen.
— *Paternoster*

Weeks

Lord Jesus Christ, Son of God,
have mercy upon me, a sinner.
— *The Jesus Prayer*

Following the seventh bead:
Glory be to the Father, and to the Son,
and to the Holy Spirit.
As it was in the beginning, is now,
and ever shall be, world without end. Amen.

Dimissory

Lord, now let your servant depart in peace,
according to your word.

For my eyes have seen your salvation,
which you have prepared before the face of all people,
to be a light to lighten the gentiles,
and to be the glory of your people, Israel.
— *Nunc dimittis, Luke 2:29-32*^{◊†}

In the name of the Father, and of the Son,
and of the Holy Spirit. **Amen.**

∾

AVE MARIA

Cross

In the name of the Father, and of the Son,
and of the Holy Spirit. **Amen.**

I believe in God,
the Father almighty,
creator of heaven and earth;
I believe in Jesus Christ, his only Son, our Lord.
He was conceived by the power of the Holy Spirit
and born of the Virgin Mary.
He suffered under Pontius Pilate,
was crucified, died, and was buried.
He descended to the dead.
On the third day he rose again.
He ascended into heaven,
and is seated at the right hand of the Father.
He will come again to judge the living and the dead.
I believe in the Holy Spirit,
the holy catholic Church,
the communion of saints,
the forgiveness of sins,

the resurrection of the body,
and the life everlasting. Amen.
— *The Apostles' Creed*◊

Invitatory

Our Father,
who art in heaven,
hallowed be thy name.
Thy kingdom come;
thy will be done
on earth as it is in heaven.
Give us this day our daily bread,
and forgive us our trespasses
as we forgive those who trespass against us.
And lead us not into temptation,
but deliver us from evil.
For thine is the kingdom,
and the power, and the glory,
for ever and ever. Amen.

Hail Mary, full of grace!
The Lord is with you.
Blessed are you amongst women,
and blessed is the fruit of your womb, Jesus.
Holy Mary, Mother of God,
pray for us sinners,
now and at the hour of our death.
— *Ave Maria*

Glory be to the Father, and to the Son,
and to the Holy Spirit.
As it was in the beginning, is now,
and ever shall be, world without end. Amen.
— *Gloria Patri*

Cruciform

Our Father,
who art in heaven,
hallowed be thy name.
Thy kingdom come;
thy will be done
on earth as it is in heaven.
Give us this day our daily bread,
and forgive us our trespasses
as we forgive those who trespass against us.
And lead us not into temptation,
but deliver us from evil.
For thine is the kingdom,
and the power, and the glory,
for ever and ever. Amen.

Weeks

Hail Mary, full of grace!
The Lord is with you.
Blessed are you amongst women,
and blessed is the fruit of your womb, Jesus.
Holy Mary, Mother of God,
pray for us sinners,
now and at the hour of our death.

Following the seventh bead:
Glory be to the Father, and to the Son,
and to the Holy Spirit.
As it was in the beginning, is now,
and ever shall be, world without end. Amen.

Dimissory

Hail, holy Queen, Mother of Mercy;
hail our life, our sweetness, and our hope.
To you do we cry,
poor banished children of Eve;
to you do we send up our sighs,
mourning and weeping in this vale of tears.
Turn then, most gracious advocate,
your eyes of mercy toward us;
and after this our exile,
show unto us the blessed fruit of your womb, Jesus.
O clement, O loving,
O sweet Virgin Mary.
Pray for us, O holy Mother of God,
that we may be made worthy of the promises of Christ.
— *Salve Regina*

In the name of the Father, and of the Son,
and of the Holy Spirit. **Amen.**

The Daily Office

As preparation for any of these daily office patterns, a confession and prayer for absolution may be made, such as:

Most merciful God,
we confess that we have sinned against you
in thought, word, and deed,
by what we have done,
and by what we have left undone.
We have not loved you with our whole heart;
we have not loved our neighbours as ourselves.
We are truly sorry and we humbly repent.
For the sake of your Son Jesus Christ,
have mercy on us and forgive us;
that we may delight in your will,
and walk in your ways,
to the glory of your Name. Amen.
— *Morning Prayer II & Evening Prayer II*◊

May almighty God have mercy on us, forgive us all our sins
through our Lord Jesus Christ, strengthen us in all goodness, and
by the power of the Holy Spirit keep us in eternal life. **Amen.**
— *Morning Prayer II & Evening Prayer II*◊†

≈

Cross

In the name of the Father, and of the Son,
and of the Holy Spirit. **Amen.**

May the words of my mouth,
and the meditation of my heart,
be always acceptable in thy sight, O Lord,
my strength, and my redeemer.
— *Psalm 19:14*‡†

O Lord, open our lips.
And our mouths shall show forth your praise.
— *Morning Prayer I*◊†

Invitatory

Come, let us sing to the Lord;
let us shout for joy to the Rock of our salvation.
Let us come before his presence with thanksgiving
and raise a loud shout to him with psalms.
For the Lord is a great God,
and a great King above all gods.
In his hand are the caverns of the earth,
and the heights of the hills are his also.
The sea is his, for he made it,
and his hands have moulded the dry land.
Come, let us bow down, and bend the knee,
and kneel before the Lord our Maker.
For he is our God,
and we are the people of his pasture
and the sheep of his hand.
Oh, that today you would hearken to his voice!
— *Venite, Psalm 95:1-7*◊

Cruciform

Our Father,
who art in heaven,
hallowed be thy name.
Thy kingdom come;
thy will be done
on earth as it is in heaven.
Give us this day our daily bread,
and forgive us our trespasses
as we forgive those who trespass against us.
And lead us not into temptation,
but deliver us from evil.
For thine is the kingdom,
and the power, and the glory,
for ever and ever. Amen.

Weeks

Surely, it is God who saves me;
I will trust in him and not be afraid.
For the Lord is my stronghold and my sure defence,
and he will be my Saviour.
— *Ecce Deus, Isaiah 12:2*$^{\diamond}$

Following the seventh bead:
Glory be to the Father, and to the Son,
and to the Holy Spirit.
As it was in the beginning, is now, and ever shall be,
world without end. Amen.

Dimissory

Show us your mercy, O Lord;
and grant us your salvation.

Clothe your ministers with righteousness;
let your people sing with joy.
Give peace, O Lord, in all the world;
for only in you can we live in safety.
Lord, keep this nation under your care;
and guide us in the way of justice and truth.
Let your way be known upon earth;
your saving health among all nations.
Let not the needy, O Lord, be forgotten;
nor the hope of the poor be taken away.
Create in us clean hearts, O God;
and sustain us with your Holy Spirit.
— *Versicles & Responses, Morning Prayer II*◊

In the name of the Father, and of the Son,
and of the Holy Spirit. **Amen.**

∾

Morning Prayer II

Cross

In the name of the Father, and of the Son,
and of the Holy Spirit. **Amen.**

The hour comes, and is now,
when the true worshipers
will worship the Father in spirit and truth,
for such the Father seeks to be his worshipers.
God is spirit, and those who worship him
must worship in spirit and truth.
— *John 4:23-24*†

O Lord, open our lips.
And our mouths shall show forth your praise.
— *Morning Prayer I*◊†

Invitatory

Be joyful in the Lord, all you lands;
serve the Lord with gladness
and come before his presence with a song.
Know this: the Lord himself is God;
he himself has made us, and we are his;
we are his people and the sheep of his pasture.
Enter his gates with thanksgiving;
go into his courts with praise;
give thanks to him and call upon his Name.
For the Lord is good;
his mercy is everlasting;
and his faithfulness endures from age to age.
— *Jubilate, Psalm 100*$^\Diamond$

Cruciform

Seek the Lord while he wills to be found;
call upon him when he draws near.
Let the wicked forsake their ways
and the evil ones their thoughts;
and let them turn to the Lord, and he will have compassion,
and to our God, for he will richly pardon.
— *Isaiah 55:6-7*$^\Diamond$

Weeks

The Lord will be your everlasting light,
and your God will be your glory.
— *Surge illuminare, Isaiah 60:19*$^\Diamond$

Following the seventh bead:
Glory be to the Father, and to the Son,
and to the Holy Spirit.

As it was in the beginning, is now,
and ever shall be, world without end. Amen.

Dimissory

Save your people, Lord, and bless your inheritance;
govern and uphold them, now and always.
Day by day we bless you;
we praise your name for ever.
Lord, keep us from all sin today;
have mercy upon us, Lord, have mercy.
Lord, show us your love and mercy;
for we put our trust in you.
In you, Lord, is our hope;
and we shall never hope in vain.
— *Versicles & Responses, Morning Prayer II*◊

In the name of the Father, and of the Son,
and of the Holy Spirit. **Amen.**

MORNING PRAYER III

Cross

In the name of the Father, and of the Son,
and of the Holy Spirit. **Amen.**

You are no longer strangers and sojourners,
but fellow citizens with the saints
and members of the household of God.
— *Ephesians 2:19*◊

O Lord, open our lips.
And our mouths shall show forth your praise.
— *Morning Prayer I*◊†

Invitatory

O ruler of the universe, Lord God,
great deeds are they that you have done,
surpassing human understanding.
Your ways are ways of righteousness and truth,
O King of all the ages.
Who can fail to do you homage, Lord,
and sing the praises of your Name?
for you only are the Holy One.
All nations will draw near and fall down before you,
because your just and holy works have been revealed.
— *Magna et mirabilia, Revelation 15:3-4*$^\lozenge$

Cruciform

Splendour and honour and kingly power
are yours by right, O Lamb that was slain,
for with your blood you have redeemed for God,
from every family, language, people, and nation,
a kingdom of priests to serve our God.
— *Dignus es, Revelation 4:11, 5:9-10*$^\lozenge$

Weeks

Send out your light and your truth, that they may lead me,
and bring me to your holy hill and to your dwelling.
— *Psalm 43:3*$^\lozenge$

Following the seventh bead:
Glory be to the Father, and to the Son,
and to the Holy Spirit.
As it was in the beginning, is now,
and ever shall be, world without end. Amen.

Dimissory

Almighty God, you have given us grace
at this time with one accord
to make our common supplication to you;
and you have promised through your well-beloved Son
that when two or three are gathered together in his name
you will be in the midst of them:
fulfil now, O Lord, our desires and petitions
as may be best for us;
granting us in this world knowledge of your truth,
and in the age to come life everlasting. Amen.
— *A Prayer of St. Chrysostom*◊

In the name of the Father, and of the Son,
and of the Holy Spirit. **Amen.**

∼

Morning Prayer IV

Cross

In the name of the Father, and of the Son,
and of the Holy Spirit. **Amen.**

You shall draw water with rejoicing
from the springs of salvation.
And on that day you shall say,
"Give thanks to the Lord and call upon his Name."
— *Ecce Deus, Isaiah 12:3-4*◊

O Lord, open our lips.
And our mouths shall show forth your praise.
— *Morning Prayer I*◊†

Invitatory

Glorify the Lord, all you works of the Lord:
praise him and highly exalt him for ever.
In the firmament of his power, glorify the Lord:
praise him and highly exalt him for ever.
Let the people of God glorify the Lord:
praise him and highly exalt him for ever.
Glorify the Lord, O priests and servants of the Lord:
praise him and highly exalt him for ever.
Let us glorify the Lord: Father, Son, and Holy Spirit:
praise him and highly exalt him for ever.
In the firmament of his power, glorify the Lord:
praise him and highly exalt him for ever.
— *The Song of the Three Young Men 35-36, 61-62*◊

Cruciform

You, my child, shall be called the prophet of the Most High,
for you will go before the Lord to prepare his way,
to give his people knowledge of salvation
by the forgiveness of their sins.
In the tender compassion of our God
the dawn from on high shall break upon us,
to shine on those who dwell in darkness
and the shadow of death,
and to guide our feet into the way of peace.
— *Benedictus Dominus Deus, Luke 1:76-79*◊

Weeks

Glory to God in the highest
and peace to his people on earth.
— *Gloria in excelsis*◊

Following the seventh bead:
Glory be to the Father, and to the Son,
and to the Holy Spirit.
As it was in the beginning, is now,
and ever shall be, world without end. Amen.

Dimissory

Heavenly Father,
in you we live and move and have our being:
we humbly pray you so to guide
and govern us by your Holy Spirit,
that in all the cares and occupations of our life
we may not forget you,
but may remember that we are ever walking in your sight;
through Jesus Christ our Lord.
— *A Collect for Guidance, Morning Prayer II*◊

In the name of the Father, and of the Son,
and of the Holy Spirit. **Amen.**

MORNING PRAYER V (PARTICULARLY SUITED FOR EASTER SEASON)

Cross

In the name of the Father, and of the Son,
and of the Holy Spirit. **Amen.**

Alleluia! Christ is risen.
The Lord is risen indeed. Alleluia!
— *The Easter Acclamation*◊

or

On this day the Lord has acted;
we will rejoice and be glad in it.
— *Psalm 118:24*◊

Then:

O Lord, open our lips.
And our mouths shall show forth your praise.
— *Morning Prayer I*◊†

Invitatory

Alleluia. Christ our Passover has been sacrificed for us;
therefore let us keep the feast,
not with the old leaven, the leaven of malice and evil,
but with the unleavened bread of sincerity and truth. Alleluia.
Christ being raised from the dead will never die again;
death no longer has dominion over him.
The death that he died, he died to sin, once for all;
but the life he lives, he lives to God.
So also consider yourselves dead to sin,
and alive to God in Jesus Christ our Lord. Alleluia.
Christ has been raised from the dead,
the first fruits of those who have fallen asleep.
For since by a man came death,
by a man has come also the resurrection of the dead.
For as in Adam all die,
so also in Christ shall all be made alive. Alleluia.
— *Pascha nostrum; 1 Corinthians 5:7-8, Romans 6:9-11, 1 Corinthians 15:20-22*◊

Cruciform

You, Christ, are the king of glory,
the eternal Son of the Father.
When you became man to set us free,
you did not shun the Virgin's womb.

26

You overcame the sting of death
and opened the kingdom of heaven to all believers.
— *Te Deum laudamus*◊

Weeks

Come, then, Lord, and help your people,
and bring us with your saints to glory everlasting.
— *Te Deum laudamus*◊

Following the seventh bead:
Glory be to the Father, and to the Son,
and to the Holy Spirit.
**As it was in the beginning, is now,
and ever shall be, world without end. Amen.**

Dimissory

Lord God, almighty and everlasting Father,
**you have brought us in safety to this new day:
preserve us with your mighty power,
that we may not fall into sin,
nor be overcome by adversity; and in all we do,
direct us to the fulfilling of your purpose;
through Jesus Christ our Lord.**
— *A Collect for Grace, Morning Prayer II*◊

In the name of the Father, and of the Son,
and of the Holy Spirit. **Amen.**

EVENING PRAYER I

Cross

In the name of the Father, and of the Son,
and of the Holy Spirit. **Amen.**

I believe in God,
the Father almighty,
creator of heaven and earth;
I believe in Jesus Christ, his only Son, our Lord.
He was conceived by the power of the Holy Spirit
and born of the Virgin Mary.
He suffered under Pontius Pilate,
was crucified, died, and was buried.
He descended to the dead.
On the third day he rose again.
He ascended into heaven,
and is seated at the right hand of the Father.
He will come again to judge the living and the dead.
I believe in the Holy Spirit,
the holy catholic Church,
the communion of saints,
the forgiveness of sins,
the resurrection of the body,
and the life everlasting. Amen.
— *The Apostles' Creed*◊

Invitatory

Let my prayer be set forth in your sight as incense,
the lifting up of my hands as the evening sacrifice.
—*Psalm 141:2*◊

O God, make speed to save us.
O Lord, make haste to help us.
— *Evening Prayer II*◊

Cruciform

I will bless the Lord who gives me counsel;
my heart teaches me, night after night.
I have set the Lord always before me;
because he is at my right hand, I shall not fall.
— *Psalm 16:7-8*◊

Weeks

Be our light in the darkness, O Lord.
Be our light in the darkness, O Lord.
— *A Collect for Aid against Perils*◊

Following the seventh bead:
Glory be to the Father, and to the Son,
and to the Holy Spirit.
As it was in the beginning, is now,
and ever shall be, world without end. Amen.

Dimissory

Show us your mercy, O Lord;
and grant us your salvation.
Clothe your ministers with righteousness;
let your people sing with joy.
Give peace, O Lord, in all the world;
for only in you can we live in safety.
Lord, keep this nation under your care;
and guide us in the way of justice and truth.
Let your way be known upon earth;
your saving health among all nations.
Let not the needy, O Lord, be forgotten;
nor the hope of the poor be taken away.

Create in us clean hearts, O God;
and sustain us with your Holy Spirit.
— *Versicles & Responses, Evening Prayer II*◊

In the name of the Father, and of the Son,
and of the Holy Spirit. **Amen.**

∼

Cross

In the name of the Father, and of the Son,
and of the Holy Spirit. **Amen.**

Seek him who made the Pleiades and Orion,
and turns deep darkness into the morning,
and darkens the day into night;
who calls for the waters of the sea
and pours them out upon the surface of the earth:
the Lord is his name.
— *Amos 5:8*◊

O God, make speed to save us.
O Lord, make haste to help us.
— *Evening Prayer II*◊

Invitatory

O gracious Light,
pure brightness of the everliving Father in heaven,
O Jesus Christ, holy and blessed!
Now as we come to the setting of the sun,
and our eyes behold the vesper light,
we sing your praises, O God: Father, Son, and Holy Spirit.

You are worthy at all times to be praised by happy voices,
O Son of God, O Giver of life,
and to be glorified through all the worlds.
— *Phos hilaron*◊

Cruciform

Our Father,
who art in heaven,
hallowed be thy name.
Thy kingdom come;
thy will be done
on earth as it is in heaven.
Give us this day our daily bread,
and forgive us our trespasses
as we forgive those who trespass against us.
And lead us not into temptation,
but deliver us from evil.
For thine is the kingdom,
and the power, and the glory,
for ever and ever. Amen.

Weeks

May the God of hope fill us
with all joy and peace in believing.
— *Romans 15:13*◊

Following the seventh bead:
Glory be to the Father, and to the Son,
and to the Holy Spirit.
As it was in the beginning, is now,
and ever shall be, world without end. Amen.

Dimissory

Almighty God, you have given us grace
at this time with one accord
to make our common supplication to you;
and you have promised through your well-beloved Son
that when two or three are gathered together in his name
you will be in the midst of them:
fulfil now, O Lord, our desires and petitions
as may be best for us;
granting us in this world knowledge of your truth,
and in the age to come life everlasting. Amen.
— *A Prayer of St. Chrysostom*[◊]

In the name of the Father, and of the Son,
and of the Holy Spirit. **Amen.**

≈

Cross

In the name of the Father, and of the Son,
and of the Holy Spirit. **Amen.**

Yours is the day, O God, yours also the night;
you established the moon and the sun.
You fixed all the boundaries of the earth;
you made both summer and winter.
— *Psalm 74:15-16*[◊]

O God, make speed to save us.
O Lord, make haste to help us.
— *Evening Prayer II*[◊]

Invitatory

My soul proclaims the greatness of the Lord,
and my spirit rejoices in God my Saviour;
for he has looked with favour on his lowly servant;
from this day all generations will call me blessed.
The Almighty has done great things for me,
and holy is his Name.
He has mercy on those who fear him
throughout all generations.
He has shown the strength of his arm;
he has scattered the proud in the imagination of their hearts.
He has cast down the mighty from their thrones,
and has lifted up the humble and meek.
He has filled the hungry with good things,
and the rich he has sent empty away.
He has come to the help of his servant Israel,
for he has remembered his promise of mercy:
the promise he made to our forebears,
to Abraham and his seed for ever.
— *Magnificat, Luke 1:46-55*◊†

Cruciform

Keep watch, dear Lord,
with those who work, or watch, or weep this night,
and give your angels charge over those who sleep.
Tend the sick, Lord Christ;
give rest to the weary, bless the dying,
soothe the suffering, pity the afflicted,
shield the joyous;
and all for your love's sake. Amen.
— *Evening Prayer II*◊

Weeks

I am the light of the world; whoever follows me
will not walk in darkness, but will have the light of life.
— *John 8:12*[◊]

Following the seventh bead:
Glory be to the Father, and to the Son,
and to the Holy Spirit.
As it was in the beginning, is now,
and ever shall be, world without end. Amen.

Dimissory

That this evening may be holy, good, and peaceful,
we entreat you, O Lord.
That your holy angels may lead us in paths of peace and
goodwill,
we entreat you, O Lord.
That we may be pardoned and forgiven for our sins and offences,
we entreat you, O Lord.
That there may be peace to your Church and to the whole world,
we entreat you, O Lord.
That we may depart this life in your faith and fear, and not be
condemned before the great judgement seat of Christ,
we entreat you, O Lord.
That we may be bound together by your Holy Spirit in the
communion of *(St. _____, and)* all your saints, entrusting one
another and all our life to Christ,
we entreat you, O Lord.
— *Versicles & Responses, Evening Prayer II*[◊]

Let us bless the Lord.
Thanks be to God.
— *Evening Prayer II*[◊]

In the name of the Father, and of the Son,
and of the Holy Spirit. **Amen.**

≈

Cross

In the name of the Father, and of the Son,
and of the Holy Spirit. **Amen.**

If I say, "Surely the darkness will cover me,
and the light around me turn to night,"
darkness is not dark to you, O Lord;
the night is as bright as the day;
darkness and light to you are both alike.
— *Psalm 139:10-11*◊

O God, make speed to save us.
O Lord, make haste to help us.
— *Evening Prayer II*◊

Invitatory

Lord Jesus, stay with us,
for evening is at hand and the day is past;
be our companion in the way,
kindle our hearts, and awaken hope,
that we may know you as you are revealed
in scripture and the breaking of bread.
Grant this for the sake of your love.
— *A Collect for the Presence of Christ, Evening Prayer II*◊

Cruciform

Be our light in the darkness, O Lord,
and in your great mercy defend us
from all perils and dangers of this night;
for the love of your only Son,
our Saviour Jesus Christ.
— *A Collect for Aid against Perils, Evening Prayer II*$^\Diamond$

Weeks

Send forth upon us the spirit of love,
that your abounding grace may increase among us.
— *Evening Prayer II*$^\Diamond$

Following the seventh bead:
Glory be to the Father, and to the Son,
and to the Holy Spirit.
As it was in the beginning, is now,
and ever shall be, world without end. Amen.

Dimissory

Lord, now let your servant depart in peace,
according to your word.
For my eyes have seen your salvation,
which you have prepared before the face of all people,
to be a light to lighten the gentiles,
and to be the glory of your people, Israel.
— *Nunc dimittis, Luke 2:29-32*$^{\Diamond\dagger}$

In the name of the Father, and of the Son,
and of the Holy Spirit. **Amen.**

≈

Cross

In the name of the Father, and of the Son,
and of the Holy Spirit. **Amen.**

From the rising of the sun to its setting
my Name shall be great among the nations,
and in every place
shall incense be offered to my Name,
and a pure offering;
for my Name shall be great among the nations,
says the Lord of Hosts.
— *Malachi 1:11*◊†

Invitatory

When the Lord restored the fortunes of Zion,
then were we like those who dream.
Then was our mouth filled with laughter
and our tongue with shouts of joy.
Then they said among the nations:
"The Lord has done great things for them."
The Lord has done great things for us,
and we are glad indeed.
— *Psalm 126:1-4*◊

Cruciform

Your word is a lantern to my feet
and a light upon my path.
Your decrees are my inheritance for ever;
truly, they are the joy of my heart.
— *Psalm 119:105, 111*◊

Weeks

If anyone is in Christ
he is a new creation;
the old has passed away,
behold the new has come.
— *2 Corinthians 5:17*◊

Following the seventh bead:
Glory be to the Father, and to the Son,
and to the Holy Spirit.
As it was in the beginning, is now,
and ever shall be, world without end. Amen.

Dimissory

Heavenly Father, send your Holy Spirit into our hearts
to direct and rule us according to your will,
to comfort us in all our afflictions,
to defend us from all error,
and to lead us into all truth;
through Jesus Christ our Lord. Amen.
— *Noonday Prayer*◊

In the name of the Father, and of the Son,
and of the Holy Spirit. **Amen.**

∾

COMPLINE I

Cross

In the name of the Father, and of the Son,
and of the Holy Spirit. **Amen.**

The Lord Almighty grant us a peaceful night and a perfect end.

Our help is in the name of the Lord,
the maker of heaven and earth.
— *Compline*◊

Invitatory

I will lay me down in peace and sleep,
for you alone, Lord, make me dwell in safety.
— *Psalm 4:8*‡†

Cruciform

Guide us while waking, O Lord,
and guard us while sleeping,
that awake we may watch with Christ,
and asleep we may rest in peace.
— *Compline*◊

Weeks

Bless the Lord, all you servants of the Lord,
you that stand by night in the house of the Lord.
— *Psalm 134:1*◊

Following the seventh bead:
Glory be to the Father, and to the Son,
and to the Holy Spirit.
As it was in the beginning, is now,
and ever shall be, world without end. Amen.

Dimissory

Into your hand, O Lord, I commend my spirit;
for you have redeemed me, O Lord, O God of truth.

Keep me, O Lord, as the apple of your eye;
hide me under the shadow of your wings.
— *Compline*^{◊†}

The almighty and merciful Lord,
Father, Son, and Holy Spirit,
bless us and keep us. **Amen.**
— *Compline*[◊]

Compline II

Cross

In the name of the Father, and of the Son,
and of the Holy Spirit. **Amen.**

The Lord Almighty grant us a peaceful night and a perfect end.

Our help is in the name of the Lord,
the maker of heaven and earth.
— *Compline*[◊]

Invitatory

I will lay me down in peace and sleep,
for you alone, Lord, make me dwell in safety.
— *Psalm 4:8*^{‡†}

Cruciform

Look down, O Lord, from your heavenly throne,
and illumine this night with your celestial brightness;

that by night as by day
your people may glorify your holy Name;
through Jesus Christ our Lord.
— *Compline*◊

Weeks

He who dwells in the shelter of the Most High
abides under the shadow of the Almighty.
— *Psalm 91:1*◊

Following the seventh bead:
Glory be to the Father, and to the Son,
and to the Holy Spirit.
As it was in the beginning, is now,
and ever shall be, world without end. Amen.

Dimissory

Visit this place, O Lord,
and drive far from it all snares of the enemy;
let your holy angels dwell with us to preserve us in peace;
and let your blessing be upon us always;
through Jesus Christ our Lord.
— *Compline*◊

The almighty and merciful Lord,
Father, Son, and Holy Spirit,
bless us and keep us. **Amen.**
— *Compline*◊

Seasonal Prayers

ADVENT

Cross

In the name of the Father, and of the Son,
and of the Holy Spirit. **Amen.**

My soul proclaims the greatness of the Lord,
and my spirit rejoices in God my Saviour;
for he has looked with favour on his lowly servant;
from this day all generations will call me blessed.
The Almighty has done great things for me,
and holy is his Name.
He has mercy on those who fear him
throughout all generations.
He has shown the strength of his arm;
he has scattered the proud in the imagination of their hearts.
He has cast down the mighty from their thrones,
and has lifted up the humble and meek.
He has filled the hungry with good things,
and the rich he has sent empty away.
He has come to the help of his servant Israel,
for he has remembered his promise of mercy:

the promise he made to our forebears,
to Abraham and his seed for ever.
— *Magnificat, Luke 1:46-55*◊†

Invitatory

The Spirit of the Lord is upon me,
because he has anointed me
to preach good news to the poor,
to bind up the broken-hearted,
to proclaim liberty to the captives
and release to those who are bound,
to proclaim the year of the Lord's favour.
— *Isaiah 61:1-2*†

Cruciform

When the Lord restored the fortunes of Zion,
then were we like those who dream.
Then was our mouth filled with laughter
and our tongue with shouts of joy.
Then they said among the nations:
"The Lord has done great things for them."
The Lord has done great things for us,
and we are glad indeed.
Restore our fortunes, O Lord,
like the watercourses of the Negev.
Those who sowed with tears
will reap with songs of joy.
— *Psalm 126:1-5*◊

Weeks

I am the voice that cries out in the wilderness,
"Prepare ye the way of the Lord!

Make straight his paths:
a highway for our God!"
— *John 1:23[†]; Isaiah 40:3[†]*

Following the seventh bead:
Glory be to the Father, and to the Son,
and to the Holy Spirit.
As it was in the beginning, is now,
and ever shall be, world without end. Amen.

Dimissory

Rejoice always.
Pray without ceasing.
In everything give thanks,
for this is the will of God in Christ Jesus toward you.
Quench not the Spirit.
Despise not the prophecies.
Test all things,
and hold firmly to that which is good.
And may the God of peace himself sanctify you in all things.
He who calls you is faithful.
— *1 Thessalonians 5:16-21, 23, 24[†]*

In the name of the Father, and of the Son,
and of the Holy Spirit. **Amen.**

∾

CHRISTMAS

Cross

In the name of the Father, and of the Son,
and of the Holy Spirit. **Amen.**

Hail Mary, full of grace!
The Lord is with you.
Blessed are you amongst women,
and blessed is the fruit of your womb, Jesus.
Holy Mary, Mother of God,
pray for us sinners,
now and at the hour of our death.

or

Hail Mary, full of grace!
The Lord is with you.
Blessed are you amongst women,
and blessed is the fruit of your womb, Jesus.
The Holy Spirit will come over you;
and the power of the Most High will overshadow you.
Therefore he who is born from you
will be called the Son of God.
— *Ave Maria; Luke 1:35, 42*[†]

Invitatory

O come, all ye faithful,
joyful and triumphant;
O come ye, O come ye
to Bethlehem.
Come and adore him,
born the King of Angels.
O come, let us adore him;
O come, let us adore him;
O come, let us adore him,
Christ the Lord.
— *Adeste fidelis, Latin hymn*

Cruciform

You have multiplied the nation.
You have increased their joy.
For unto us a child is born;
unto us a son is given;
and the government will be on his shoulders.
His name will be called Wonderful Counsellor,
Mighty God, Everlasting Father,
Prince of Peace.
— *Isaiah 9:3, 6*[†]

Weeks

Glory to God in the highest,
and on earth peace, good will toward all.
The Word was made flesh and dwelt among us.
— *Luke 2:14, John 1:14*[†]

Following the seventh bead:
Glory be to the Father, and to the Son,
and to the Holy Spirit.
As it was in the beginning, is now,
and ever shall be, world without end. Amen.

Dimissory

My soul proclaims the greatness of the Lord,
and my spirit rejoices in God my Saviour;
for he has looked with favour on his lowly servant;
from this day all generations will call me blessed.
The Almighty has done great things for me,
and holy is his Name.
He has mercy on those who fear him
throughout all generations.

He has shown the strength of his arm;
he has scattered the proud in the imagination of their hearts.
He has cast down the mighty from their thrones,
and has lifted up the humble and meek.
He has filled the hungry with good things,
and the rich he has sent empty away.
He has come to the help of his servant Israel,
for he has remembered his promise of mercy:
the promise he made to our forebears,
to Abraham and his seed for ever.
— *Magnificat, Luke 1:46-55*^{◊†}

In the name of the Father, and of the Son,
and of the Holy Spirit. **Amen.**

∾

Epiphany

Cross

In the name of the Father, and of the Son,
and of the Holy Spirit. **Amen.**

The people who walked in darkness have seen a great light.
The light has shined on those
who dwelled in the shadow of death.
You have multiplied the nation.
You have increased their joy.
For unto us a child is born;
unto us a son is given.
— *Isaiah 9:2-3, 6*[†]

Invitatory

Arise, shine; for your light has come,
and the Lord's glory has risen on you.

For, behold, darkness will cover the earth,
and thick darkness the peoples;
but the Lord will arise on you,
and his glory shall be seen on you.
Nations will come to your light,
and kings to the brightness of your rising.
— *Isaiah 60:1-3*

Cruciform

You Bethlehem, in the land of Judah,
are in no way least among the princes of Judah;
for out of you shall come a ruler
who shall shepherd my people, Israel.
— *Matthew 2:6*[†]

Weeks

Where is he who is born King of the Jews?
For we saw his star in the east,
and have come to worship him.
— *Matthew 2:2*

Following the seventh bead:
Glory be to the Father, and to the Son,
and to the Holy Spirit.
As it was in the beginning, is now,
and ever shall be, world without end. Amen.

Dimissory

O gracious Light,
pure brightness of the everliving Father in heaven,
O Jesus Christ, holy and blessed!

Now as we come to the setting of the sun,
and our eyes behold the vesper light,
we sing your praises, O God: Father, Son, and Holy Spirit.
You are worthy at all times to be praised by happy voices,
O Son of God, O Giver of life,
and to be glorified through all the worlds.
— *Phos hilaron*◊

In the name of the Father, and of the Son,
and of the Holy Spirit. **Amen.**

∾

Ash Wednesday

*For solo prayer, "we / us" may be changed to "I / me" in the opening
confession and the concluding prayer for absolution.*

Cross

In the name of the Father, and of the Son,
and of the Holy Spirit. **Amen.**

Most holy and merciful Father:
we confess to you and to one another,
and to the whole communion of saints
in heaven and on earth,
that we have sinned by our own fault,
in thought, word, and deed;
by what we have done,
and by what we have left undone.
We have not loved you with our whole heart,
and mind, and strength.
We have not loved our neighbours as ourselves.
We have not forgiven others, as we have been forgiven.
Accept our repentance,
and restore us, good Lord.

Accomplish in us the work of your salvation,
that we may show forth your glory in the world.
— *from the adapted Confiteor, Ash Wednesday*[◊]

Invitatory

Blow the trumpet in Zion,
and sound an alarm in my holy mountain!
For the day of the Lord comes,
for it is close at hand.
Rend your hearts and not your garments,
and turn to the Lord, your God;
for he is gracious and merciful,
slow to anger, and abundant in loving kindness.
Blow the trumpet in Zion!
Sanctify a fast.
Call a solemn assembly.
Gather the people.
Sanctify the assembly.
Assemble the elders.
Let the priests weep between the porch and the altar,
and let them say, "Spare your people, O Lord."
— *Joel 2:1-2, 13b, 15-17*[*]; *v. 13a*[◊]

Cruciform

When you pray, do not be as the hypocrites,
for they love to stand and pray and be seen.
Truly I tell you, they have received their reward.
When you fast, do not be like the hypocrites, with sad faces.
For they disfigure their faces that they may be seen.
Truly I tell you, they have received their reward.
But you, when you fast, anoint your head and wash your face,
so that you are not seen by men.
And your Father, who sees in secret, will reward you.
— *Matthew 6:5, 16-18*[†]

Weeks

At an acceptable time I listened to you.
In a day of salvation I helped you.
— 2 Corinthians 6:2

Following the seventh bead:
Glory be to the Father, and to the Son,
and to the Holy Spirit.
As it was in the beginning, is now,
and ever shall be, world without end. Amen.

Dimissory

Have mercy on me, God,
according to your loving kindness.
According to the multitude of your tender mercies,
blot out my transgressions.
Wash me thoroughly from my iniquity.
Cleanse me from my sin.
For I know my transgressions.
My sin is constantly before me.
Against you, and you only, I have sinned,
and done what is evil in your sight,
so you may be proved right when you speak,
and justified when you judge.
Behold, I was born in iniquity.
My mother conceived me in sin.
Behold, you desire truth in the inward parts.
You teach me wisdom in the inmost place.
Purify me with hyssop, and I will be clean.
Wash me, and I will be whiter than snow.
Create in me a clean heart, O God;
and renew a right spirit within me.
— Psalm 51:1-7*†; v. 10*

May almighty God have mercy on us, forgive us all our sins
through our Lord Jesus Christ, strengthen us in all goodness, and
by the power of the Holy Spirit keep us in eternal life. **Amen.**
— *Morning Prayer II & Evening Prayer II*[◊†]

In the name of the Father, and of the Son,
and of the Holy Spirit. **Amen.**

∾

Lent

*For solo prayer, "we / us" may be changed to "I / me" in the opening
confession and the concluding prayer for absolution.*

Cross

In the name of the Father, and of the Son,
and of the Holy Spirit. **Amen.**

Most holy and merciful Father:
we confess to you and to one another,
and to the whole communion of saints
in heaven and on earth,
that we have sinned by our own fault,
in thought, word, and deed;
by what we have done,
and by what we have left undone.
We have not loved you with our whole heart,
and mind, and strength.
We have not loved our neighbours as ourselves.
We have not forgiven others, as we have been forgiven.
Accept our repentance,
and restore us, good Lord.
Accomplish in us the work of your salvation,
that we may show forth your glory in the world.
— *from the adapted Confiteor, Ash Wednesday*[◊]

Invitatory

To you, O Lord, I lift up my soul.
My God, I have trusted in you; let me not be shamed.
Lord, remember your tender mercies and your loving kindness,
for they are from old times.
Do not remember the sins of my youth, nor my transgressions.
Remember me according to your loving kindness,
for your goodness' sake, O Lord.
Good and upright is the Lord;
therefore he will instruct sinners in the way.
He will guide the humble in justice.
He will teach the humble his way.
— *Psalm 25:1-2, 6-9*

Cruciform

"Behold, the days will come," says the Lord,
"that I will make a new covenant.
I will put my law in your inmost parts,
and I will write it in your heart.
I will be your God,
and you shall be my people."
— *Jeremiah 31:31, 33*[†]

Weeks

God sent not his Son to condemn the world,
but that through him the world might be saved.
— *John 3:17*[†]

Following the seventh bead:
Glory be to the Father, and to the Son,
and to the Holy Spirit.
As it was in the beginning, is now,
and ever shall be, world without end. Amen.

Dimissory

Let me hear joy and gladness,
that the bones which you have broken may rejoice.
Hide your face from my sins,
and blot out all my iniquities.
Create in me a clean heart, O God;
and renew a right spirit within me.
Cast me not away from your presence,
and take not your holy spirit from me.
Restore unto me the joy of your salvation;
and uphold me with a willing spirit.
— *Psalm 51:8-9*⁕†; *vv. 10-12*⁕†

May almighty God have mercy on us, forgive us all our sins
through our Lord Jesus Christ, strengthen us in all goodness, and
by the power of the Holy Spirit keep us in eternal life. **Amen.**
— *Morning Prayer II & Evening Prayer II*◊†

Cross

In the name of the Father, and of the Son,
and of the Holy Spirit. **Amen.**

Hosanna to the Son of David!
Blessed is he who comes in the name of the Lord!
Hosanna in the highest!
— *Matthew 21:9*

Invitatory

Give thanks to the Lord, for he is good,
for his loving kindness endures forever.
Let Israel now say
that his loving kindness endures forever.
Open to me the gates of righteousness.
I will enter into them.
I will give thanks to the Lord.
This is the gate of the Lord;
the righteous will enter into it.
I will give thanks to you, for you have answered me,
and have become my salvation.
The stone which the builders rejected
has become the cornerstone.
This is the Lord's doing.
It is marvellous in our eyes.
This is the day that the Lord has made.
We will rejoice and be glad in it!
O give thanks to the Lord, for he is good,
for his loving kindness endures forever.
— *Psalm 118:1-2, 19-24, 29*

Cruciform

Rejoice greatly, O daughter of Zion!
Shout, O daughter of Jerusalem!
Behold, your King comes to you!
He is righteous, and having salvation;
lowly, and riding on a donkey,
even on a colt, the foal of a donkey.
— *Zechariah 9:9, cf. John 12:15*

Weeks

Blessed is the King who comes in the name of the Lord!
Peace in heaven and glory in the highest!
— *Luke 19:38*◊

Following the seventh bead:
Glory be to the Father, and to the Son,
and to the Holy Spirit.
As it was in the beginning, is now,
and ever shall be, world without end. Amen.

Dimissory

Be joyful in the Lord, all you lands;
serve the Lord with gladness
and come before his presence with a song.
Know this: the Lord himself is God;
he himself has made us, and we are his;
we are his people and the sheep of his pasture.
Enter his gates with thanksgiving;
go into his courts with praise;
give thanks to him and call upon his Name.
For the Lord is good;
his mercy is everlasting;
and his faithfulness endures from age to age.
— *Jubilate, Psalm 100*◊

In the name of the Father, and of the Son,
and of the Holy Spirit. **Amen.**

∽

Cross

In the name of the Father, and of the Son,
and of the Holy Spirit. **Amen.**

Is it nothing to you, all you who pass by?
Look and see if there is any sorrow like my sorrow
which was brought upon me,
whom the Lord hath afflicted.
— *Lamentations 1:12*◊

Invitatory

Remember not, Lord Christ, our offences,
nor the offences of our forefathers;
neither reward us according to our sins.
Spare us, good Lord, spare thy people,
whom thou hast redeemed with thy most precious blood,
and by thy mercy preserve us, for ever.
Spare us, good Lord.
Spare us, good Lord.
— *The Great Litany*◊

Cruciform

O Lamb of God, who takes away the sins of the world:
have mercy upon us.
O Lamb of God, who takes away the sins of the world:
have mercy upon us.
O Lamb of God, who takes away the sins of the world:
grant us your peace.
— *Agnus Dei*◊†

Weeks

Pray these prayers in order, one for each bead.

1. From all evil and wickedness; from sin; from the crafts and assaults of the devil; and from everlasting damnation,
Good Lord, deliver us.

2. From all blindness of heart; from pride, vainglory, and hypocrisy; from envy, hatred, and malice; and from all want of charity,
Good Lord, deliver us.

3. From all inordinate and sinful affections; and from all the deceits of the world, the flesh, and the devil,
Good Lord, deliver us.

4. From all false doctrine, heresy, and schism; from hardness of heart, and contempt of thy Word and commandment,
Good Lord, deliver us.

5. From lightning and tempest; from earthquake, fire, and flood; from plague, pestilence, and famine,
Good Lord, deliver us.

6. From all oppression, conspiracy, and rebellion; from violence, battle, and murder; and from dying suddenly and unprepared,
Good Lord, deliver us.

7. In all time of our tribulation; in all time of our prosperity; in the hour of death, and in the day of judgment,
Good Lord, deliver us.
— *The Great Litany*◊

Following the seventh bead:
Glory be to the Father, and to the Son,
and to the Holy Spirit.

As it was in the beginning, is now,
and ever shall be, world without end. Amen.

Dimissory

From our enemies defend us, O Christ.
Graciously behold our afflictions.
With pity behold the sorrows of our hearts.
Mercifully forgive the sins of thy people.
Favourably with mercy hear our prayers.
O Son of David, have mercy upon us.
Both now and ever vouchsafe to hear us, O Christ.
Graciously hear us, O Christ;
graciously hear us, O Lord Christ.
— *The Great Litany*◊

In the name of the Father, and of the Son,
and of the Holy Spirit. **Amen.**

∾

Cross

In the name of the Father, and of the Son,
and of the Holy Spirit. **Amen.**

I love the Lord, for he listens to my voice,
and to my cries for mercy.
Because he has turned his ear to me,
I will call upon him for as long as I live.
— *Psalm 116:1-2*†

Our Father,
who art in heaven,
hallowed be thy name.

Thy kingdom come;
thy will be done
on earth as it is in heaven.
Give us this day our daily bread,
and forgive us our trespasses
as we forgive those who trespass against us.
And lead us not into temptation,
but deliver us from evil.
For thine is the kingdom,
and the power, and the glory,
for ever and ever. Amen.

Invitatory

This day shall be a memorial for you.
You shall keep it as a feast to the Lord.
You shall keep it as a feast
throughout your generations.
— *Exodus 12:14*

Cruciform

You call me "Teacher" and "Lord."
You say correctly, for so I am.
If, then, I have washed your feet,
so you should do the same.
For I have given you an example,
that you should do as I have done to you.
If you know these things,
then blessed are you if you do them.
— *John 13:13-15, 17*[†]

Weeks

A new commandment I give unto you,
that you should love one another.
Just as I have loved you,
love also one another.
— *John 13:34*†

Following the seventh bead:
Glory be to the Father, and to the Son,
and to the Holy Spirit.
As it was in the beginning, is now,
and ever shall be, world without end. Amen.

Dimissory

For I received from the Lord that which I delivered to you,
that the Lord Jesus,
on the night in which he was betrayed, took bread.
When he had given thanks, he broke it and said:
"Take, eat. This is my body, which is broken for you.
Do this in memory of me."
In the same way he also took the cup after supper, saying:
"This cup is the new covenant in my blood.
Do this, as often as you drink, in memory of me."
For as often as you eat this bread and drink this cup,
you proclaim the Lord's death until he comes.
— *1 Corinthians 11:23-26*

Christ our Passover is sacrificed for us;
therefore, let us keep the feast.
— *1 Corinthians 5:7-8*◊

In the name of the Father, and of the Son,
and of the Holy Spirit. **Amen.**

≈

GOOD FRIDAY

Cross

In the name of the Father, and of the Son,
and of the Holy Spirit. **Amen.**

My people, what have I done to you?
How have I burdened you? Answer me!
What could I have done for you that I have not done?
I brought you up out of the land of Egypt,
and redeemed you out of the house of bondage.
I gave you a royal sceptre;
and you gave my head a crown of thorns.
I exalted you with great power;
and you lifted me up upon the cross.
— *Micah 6:3-4*; the Reproaches (James Healey Willan, 1912)*

or

Were you there when they crucified my Lord?
Were you there when they crucified my Lord?
O, sometimes it causes me to tremble,
tremble,
tremble.
Were you there when they crucified my Lord?

Were you there when they nailed him to the tree?
Were you there when they nailed him to the tree?
O, sometimes it causes me to tremble,
tremble,
tremble.
Were you there when they nailed him to the tree?

Were you there when they laid him in the tomb?
Were you there when they laid him in the tomb?

O, sometimes it causes me to tremble,
tremble,
tremble.
Were you there when they laid him in the tomb?
— *African American spiritual*

Invitatory

My God, my God, why have you forsaken me?
Why are you so far from helping me,
and from the words of my groaning?
My God, I cry in the daytime, but you do not answer;
in the night season, and am not silent.
But you are holy,
you who inhabit the praises of Israel.
Our fathers trusted in you.
They trusted, and you delivered them.
They cried to you, and were delivered.
They trusted in you, and were not disappointed.
Do not be far from me, for trouble is near.
For there is no one to help.
They divide my garments among them.
They cast lots for my clothing.
But do not be far off, O Lord.
You are my help. Hurry to help me!
Deliver my soul from the sword,
my precious life from the power of the dog.
— *Psalm 22:1-5, 11, 18-20*

Cruciform

Surely he has borne our sickness
and carried our suffering;
yet we considered him plagued,
struck by God, and afflicted.
But he was pierced for our transgressions.
He was crushed for our iniquities.

The punishment that brought our peace was on him;
and by his stripes we are healed.
All we like sheep have gone astray;
we have turned every one to his own way;
and the Lord has laid upon him the iniquity of us all.
— *Isaiah 53:4-5*[#†]*, v. 6*[◊†]

Weeks

When Jesus had received the wine, he said, "It is finished."
Then he bowed his head and gave up his spirit.
— *John 19:30*

Following the seventh bead:
Glory be to the Father, and to the Son,
and to the Holy Spirit.
As it was in the beginning, is now,
and ever shall be, world without end. Amen.

Dimissory

"This is the covenant that I will make with them:
after those days," says the Lord,
"I will put my laws on their heart,
I will also write them on their mind;
I will remember their sins and their iniquities no more."
— *Hebrews 10:16-17*

Holy God,
holy and mighty,
Holy Immortal One,
have mercy upon us.
— *Trisagion*[◊]

In the name of the Father, and of the Son,
and of the Holy Spirit. **Amen.**

Cross

In the name of the Father, and of the Son,
and of the Holy Spirit. **Amen.**

I believe in God,
the Father almighty,
creator of heaven and earth;
I believe in Jesus Christ, his only Son, our Lord.
He was conceived by the power of the Holy Spirit
and born of the Virgin Mary.
He suffered under Pontius Pilate,
was crucified, died, and was buried.
He descended to the dead.
On the third day he rose again.
He ascended into heaven,
and is seated at the right hand of the Father.
He will come again to judge the living and the dead.
I believe in the Holy Spirit,
the holy catholic Church,
the communion of saints,
the forgiveness of sins,
the resurrection of the body,
and the life everlasting. Amen.
— *The Apostles' Creed*◊

Invitatory

Save your people, Lord, and bless your inheritance;
govern and uphold them, now and always.
Day by day we bless you;
we praise your name for ever.

Lord, keep us from all sin today;
have mercy upon us, Lord, have mercy.
Lord, show us your love and mercy;
for we put our trust in you.
In you, Lord, is our hope;
and we shall never hope in vain.
— *Versicles & Responses, Morning Prayer II*

Cruciform

All we like sheep have gone astray;
we have turned every one to his own way;
and the Lord has laid upon him
the iniquity of us all.
— *Isaiah 53:6*^{◊†}

Weeks

Kyrie eleison.
Christe eleison.
Kyrie eleison.

Following the seventh bead:
Glory be to the Father, and to the Son,
and to the Holy Spirit.
As it was in the beginning, is now,
and ever shall be, world without end. Amen.

Dimissory

Remember my affliction and my misery,
the wormwood and the gall.
My soul still remembers them,
and is bowed down within me.
This I recall to my mind;
therefore I have hope.

The steadfast love of the Lord never ceases;
his mercies never come to an end.
They are new every morning.
Great is your faithfulness.
"The Lord is my portion," says my soul.
"Therefore I will hope in him."
— *Lamentations 3:19*[‡]*; vv. 20-21, 24*[*]*; vv. 22-23, NRSV*

In the name of the Father, and of the Son,
and of the Holy Spirit. **Amen.**

THE EASTER VIGIL

Cross

In the name of the Father, and of the Son,
and of the Holy Spirit. **Amen.**

On this most holy night *(or* morn*)*,
we welcome the Light of Christ.
We welcome the Light of Christ.
Thanks be to God.

Invitatory

Rejoice now, heavenly hosts and choirs of angels,
and let your trumpets shout salvation
for the victory of our mighty King.
Rejoice and sing now, all the round earth,
bright with a glorious splendour,
for darkness has been vanquished by our eternal King.
Rejoice and be glad now, Mother Church,
and let your holy courts, in radiant light,
resound with the praises of your people.
— *Exultet*[◊]

Cruciform

Do not be afraid,
for I know that you seek Jesus, who was crucified.
Why do you seek the living among the dead?
Come, see the place where the Lord was lying.
— *Matthew 28:5-6*†, *Luke 24:5*

Weeks

He is not here,
for he is risen, just as he said.
— *Matthew 28:6*※

Following the seventh bead:
Glory be to the Father, and to the Son,
and to the Holy Spirit.
As it was in the beginning, is now,
and ever shall be, world without end. Amen.

Dimissory

Mary Magdalene went and announced to the disciples,
"I have seen the Lord."
— *John 20:18, NRSV*

Almighty God,
by the Passover of your Son
you have brought us out of sin into righteousness
and out of death into life.
Grant to those who are sealed by your Holy Spirit
the will and the power to proclaim you to all the world;
through Jesus Christ our Lord.
— *The Collect for Ezekiel 37:1-14, Easter Vigil*◊

In the name of the Father, and of the Son,
and of the Holy Spirit. **Amen.**

∾

Cross

Alleluia! Christ is risen.
The Lord is risen indeed. Alleluia!
— *The Easter Acclamation*[◊]

In the name of the Father, and of the Son,
and of the Holy Spirit. **Amen.**

On this mountain, the Lord of Hosts
will make the peoples a feast,
a feast of choice meat, a feast of choice wines.
He will destroy the veil spread over nations.
He has swallowed up death forever!
The Lord God will wipe away tears from all faces.
He will take the reproach of his people away,
for the Lord has spoken it.
— *Isaiah 25:6-8*

Invitatory

For I delivered to you that which I received:
that Christ died for our sins,
that he was buried,
that he was raised on the third day,
that he appeared to Cephas,
and then to the twelve.
So we preach,
and so you believed.
— *1 Corinthians 15:3-5, 11*

Cruciform

from Easter Day:
Do not be amazed.
You seek Jesus, who was crucified.
He is risen. He is not here.
Behold the place where they laid him!
— *Mark 16:6*[†]

from the Third Sunday of Easter:
The Lord breathed on them, saying:
"Peace be with you.
As the Father sent me, so I send you.
Receive the Holy Spirit!
If you forgive the sins of any,
they are forgiven."
— *John 20:21-23*[†]

from the Fifth Sunday of Easter:
Beloved, now we are children of God.
It is not yet revealed what we will be;
but we know that when he is revealed,
we will be like him;
for we will see him just as he is.
— *1 John 3:2*

Weeks

From Easter Day:
Alleluia! Christ is risen.
The Lord is risen indeed. Alleluia!
— *The Easter Acclamation*[◊]

From the Second Sunday of Easter:
"Put your finger here and see my hands. ...
Do not doubt but believe."
— *John 20:27a, 27c, NRSV*

From the Third Sunday of Easter:
See what great love the Father gives us,
that we should be called the children of God!
— *1 John 3:1*

From the Fourth Sunday of Easter:
I am the good shepherd, and I know my own,
and my own know me.
— *John 10:14*※

From the Fifth Sunday of Easter:
There is no fear in love;
but perfect love casts out fear.
— *1 John 4:18*

From the Sixth Sunday of Easter:
You did not choose me, but I chose you.
And I appointed you to go and bear fruit,
fruit that will last.
— *John 15:16, NRSV*

From the Seventh Sunday of Easter:
It is not for you to know the Kingdom's times or seasons,
but you will receive power when the Holy Spirit comes.
— *Acts 1:7-8*†

Following the seventh bead:
Glory be to the Father, and to the Son,
and to the Holy Spirit.
As it was in the beginning, is now,
and ever shall be, world without end. Amen.

Dimissory

The Lord is my strength and song.
He has become my salvation.

The voice of rejoicing and salvation
is in the tents of the righteous.
I will not die, but live,
and declare the Lord's works.
The Lord has punished me severely,
but he has not given me over to death.
Open to me the gates of righteousness.
I will enter into them. I will give thanks to the Lord.
The stone which the builders rejected
has become the cornerstone.
This is the Lord's doing.
It is marvellous in our eyes.
This is the day that the Lord has made.
We will rejoice and be glad in it!
— *Psalm 118:14-15, 17-19, 22-24*

In the name of the Father, and of the Son,
and of the Holy Spirit. **Amen.**

∾

THE KINGDOM

Cross

In the name of the Father, and of the Son,
and of the Holy Spirit. **Amen.**

For the Lord God says:
"Behold, I myself, even I, will search for my sheep,
and will seek them out.
I will deliver them out of all places
where they have been scattered.
I will bring them out from the peoples,
and gather them from the countries,
and will bring them into their own land.

I will feed them by the watercourses,
and in all the good pasture.
There they will lie down in a good fold.
They will feed on fat pasture on the mountains of Israel.
I myself will be the shepherd of my sheep,
and I will cause them to lie down," says the Lord God.
"I will seek that which was lost,
and will bring back that which was driven away,
and will bind up that which was broken."
— *Ezekiel 34:11-16*

Invitatory

Concerning the times and the seasons,
you know well that the day of the Lord
comes like a thief in the night.
You are all children of light
and children of the day.
We do not belong to the night,
nor to darkness;
so let us not sleep, as the rest do,
but let us watch and be sober.
Therefore exhort one another,
and build each other up.
— *1 Thessalonians 5:1-2, 5-6, 11*

Cruciform

Be silent at the presence of the Lord God,
for the day of the Lord is at hand.
For the Lord has prepared a sacrifice.
He has consecrated his guests.
— *Zephaniah 1:7*

Weeks

Behold, he is coming with the clouds,
and every eye will see him. Even so, amen.
— *Revelation 1:7*

Following the seventh bead:
Glory be to the Father, and to the Son,
and to the Holy Spirit.
As it was in the beginning, is now,
and ever shall be, world without end. Amen.

Dimissory

Lord, now let your servant depart in peace,
according to your word.
For my eyes have seen your salvation,
which you have prepared before the face of all people,
to be a light to lighten the gentiles,
and to be the glory of your people, Israel.
— *Nunc dimittis, Luke 2:29-32*[◊†]

In the name of the Father, and of the Son,
and of the Holy Spirit. **Amen.**

Feasts & Fasts (Moveable)

Cross

In the name of the Father, and of the Son,
and of the Holy Spirit. **Amen.**

In the beginning, God created the heavens,
and God created the earth.
God said "Let there be light", and there was light.
God saw the light, and saw that it was good.
— *Genesis 1:1, 3-4*[†]

Invitatory

Come, let us sing to the Lord;
let us shout for joy to the Rock of our salvation.
Let us come before his presence with thanksgiving
and raise a loud shout to him with psalms.
For the Lord is a great God,
and a great King above all gods.
In his hand are the caverns of the earth,
and the heights of the hills are his also.

The sea is his, for he made it,
and his hands have moulded the dry land.
Come, let us bow down, and bend the knee,
and kneel before the Lord our Maker.
For he is our God,
and we are the people of his pasture
and the sheep of his hand.
Oh, that today you would hearken to his voice!
— *Venite, Psalm 95:1-7*^◇

Cruciform

Does not wisdom cry out?
Does not understanding raise her voice?
"The Lord possessed me in the beginning,
before his deeds of old.
I was set up from everlasting,
before the earth existed."
— *Proverbs 8:1, 22-23*

Weeks

The light shines in the darkness,
and the darkness did not overcome it.
The Word became flesh, and dwelt among us.
And we have seen his glory, full of grace and truth.
— *John 1:5, 14*^†

Following the seventh bead:
Glory be to the Father, and to the Son,
and to the Holy Spirit.
As it was in the beginning, is now,
and ever shall be, world without end. Amen.

Dimissory

Worthy are you, our Lord and God, the Holy One,
to receive the glory, the honour, and the power,
for you created all things:
by your desire they came to be,
and by your will they were created!
— *Revelation 4:11*[†]

In the name of the Father, and of the Son,
and of the Holy Spirit. **Amen.**

∽

The Transfiguration: The Last Sunday before Lent

See Feasts (Fixed), 6th August.

∽

The Ascension

Cross

Alleluia! Christ is risen.
The Lord is risen indeed. Alleluia!
— *The Easter Acclamation*[◊]

In the name of the Father, and of the Son,
and of the Holy Spirit. **Amen.**

I believe in God,
the Father almighty,
creator of heaven and earth;
I believe in Jesus Christ, his only Son, our Lord.
He was conceived by the power of the Holy Spirit
and born of the Virgin Mary.

He suffered under Pontius Pilate,
was crucified, died, and was buried.
He descended to the dead.
On the third day he rose again.
He ascended into heaven,
and is seated at the right hand of the Father.
He will come again to judge the living and the dead.
I believe in the Holy Spirit,
the holy catholic Church,
the communion of saints,
the forgiveness of sins,
the resurrection of the body,
and the life everlasting. Amen.
— *The Apostles' Creed*◊

Invitatory

I have heard of your faith in the Lord Jesus,
and the love which you have toward the saints;
so I never cease giving thanks for you,
and asking in my prayers,
that the God of our Lord Jesus Christ,
the Father of glory,
may give to you a spirit of wisdom,
and enlighten the eyes of your hearts,
that you may know the hope of his calling,
and the riches of his glory.
— *Ephesians 1:15-18*†

Cruciform

While Jesus blessed them,
he withdrew from them,
and was carried up to heaven.
They worshiped him,
and returned to Jerusalem
with great joy.

They were continually in the temple,
praising and blessing God.
— *Luke 24:51-53*[†]

Weeks

It is not for you to know the Kingdom's times or seasons,
but you will receive power when the Holy Spirit comes.
— *Acts 1:7-8*[†]

Following the seventh bead:
Glory be to the Father, and to the Son,
and to the Holy Spirit.
As it was in the beginning, is now,
and ever shall be, world without end. Amen.

Dimissory

The angels said: "You men of Galilee,
why do you stand looking into the sky?
This Jesus, who was received from you,
will come back the same way
as you saw him go."
— *Acts 1:11*[†]

In the name of the Father, and of the Son,
and of the Holy Spirit. **Amen.**

PENTECOST

Cross

In the name of the Father, and of the Son,
and of the Holy Spirit. **Amen.**

Lord, how many are your works!
In wisdom, you have made them all.
The earth is full of your riches.
There is the sea, great and wide,
in which are innumerable living things,
both small and large animals.
There the ships go,
and Leviathan, whom you formed to play there.
These all wait for you,
that you may give them their food in due season.
You give to them; they gather.
You open your hand; they are satisfied with good.
You hide your face; they are troubled.
You take away their breath;
they die and return to the dust.
You send out your Spirit and they are created.
You renew the face of the ground.
Let the Lord's glory endure forever.
Let the Lord rejoice in his works.
He looks at the earth, and it trembles.
He touches the mountains, and they smoke.
I will sing to the Lord as long as I live.
I will sing praise to my God while I have any being.
Let my meditation be sweet to him.
I will rejoice in the Lord.
— *Psalm 104:24-34*

Invitatory

It will be in the last days, says God,
that I will pour out my Spirit on all flesh.
Your sons and your daughters will prophesy.
Your young men will see visions.
Your old men will dream dreams.
Yes, and on my servants and on my handmaidens in those days,
I will pour out my Spirit, and they will prophesy.

I will show wonders in the sky above,
and signs on the earth beneath:
blood, and fire, and billows of smoke.
The sun will be turned into darkness,
and the moon into blood,
before the great and glorious day of the Lord comes.
But whoever will call on the name of the Lord will be saved.
— *Acts 2:17-21, cf. Joel 2:28-32*

Cruciform

Jesus said, "Peace be with you.
As the Father sent me, so I send you."
Then he breathed on them, and said:
"Receive the Holy Spirit!
If you forgive the sins of any, they have been forgiven them.
If you retain the sins of any, they have been retained."
— *John 20:21-23*[†]

Weeks

When the Spirit of truth has come,
he will guide you into all truth.
— *John 16:13*[†]

Following the seventh bead:
Glory be to the Father, and to the Son,
and to the Holy Spirit.
As it was in the beginning, is now,
and ever shall be, world without end. Amen.

Dimissory

Arise, shine, for your light has come,
and the glory of the Lord has dawned upon you.

For behold, darkness covers the land;
deep gloom enshrouds the peoples.
But over you the Lord will rise,
and his glory will appear upon you.
Nations will stream to your light,
and kings to the brightness of your dawning.
Your gates will always be open;
by day or night they will never be shut.
They will call you, the City of the Lord,
the Zion of the Holy One of Israel.
Violence will no more be heard in your land,
ruin or destruction within your borders.
You will call your walls, Salvation,
and all your portals, Praise.
The sun will no more be your light by day;
by night you will not need the brightness of the moon.
The Lord will be your everlasting light,
and your God will be your glory.
— *Surge illuminare, Isaiah 60:1-3, 11, 14, 18-19*◊

In the name of the Father, and of the Son,
and of the Holy Spirit. **Amen.**

∼

TRINITY

Cross

In the name of the Father, and of the Son,
and of the Holy Spirit. **Amen.**

I believe in God,
the Father almighty,
creator of heaven and earth;
I believe in Jesus Christ, his only Son, our Lord.

He was conceived by the power of the Holy Spirit
and born of the Virgin Mary.
He suffered under Pontius Pilate,
was crucified, died, and was buried.
He descended to the dead.
On the third day he rose again.
He ascended into heaven,
and is seated at the right hand of the Father.
He will come again to judge the living and the dead.
I believe in the Holy Spirit,
the holy catholic Church,
the communion of saints,
the forgiveness of sins,
the resurrection of the body,
and the life everlasting. Amen.

— *The Apostles' Creed*[◊]

Invitatory

O Lord our Governor,
how exalted is your Name in all the world!
Out of the mouths of infants and children
your majesty is praised above the heavens.
You have set up a stronghold against your adversaries,
to quell the enemy and the avenger.
When I consider your heavens, the work of your fingers,
the moon and the stars you have set in their courses,
what is man that you should be mindful of him?,
the son of man that you should seek him out?
You have made him but little lower than the angels;
you adorn him with glory and honour;
you give him mastery over the works of your hands;
you put all things under his feet:
all sheep and oxen,
even the wild beasts of the field,
the birds of the air, the fish of the sea,
and whatsoever walks in the paths of the sea.

O Lord our Governor,
how exalted is your Name in all the world!
— *Psalm 8$^\Diamond$*

Cruciform

Praise God, from whom all blessings flow.
Praise him, all creatures here below.
Praise him above, ye heavenly host.
Praise Father, Son, and Holy Ghost.
— *The Doxology (Bishop Thomas Ken, 1695)*

Weeks

Go and make disciples of all nations,
baptising them in the name of
the Father, and of the Son, and of the Holy Spirit.
— *Matthew 28:19*

Following the seventh bead:
Glory be to the Father, and to the Son,
and to the Holy Spirit.
As it was in the beginning, is now,
and ever shall be, world without end. Amen.

Dimissory

Almighty and everlasting God,
you have given to us, your servants, grace,
by the confession of a true faith,
to acknowledge the glory of the eternal Trinity,
and in the power of your divine Majesty
to worship the Unity.
Keep us steadfast in this faith and worship,
and bring us at last to see you
in your one and eternal glory,

O Father; who with the Son
and the Holy Spirit live and reign,
one God, for ever and ever.
— The Collect for Trinity Sunday◊

In the name of the Father, and of the Son,
and of the Holy Spirit. **Amen.**

❧

Corpus Christi

Cross

In the name of the Father, and of the Son,
and of the Holy Spirit. **Amen.**

The Lord be with you.
And also with you.
Lift up your hearts.
We lift them to the Lord.
Let us give thanks to the Lord our God.
It is right to give him thanks and praise.
— Holy Eucharist II◊

Invitatory

What will I give to the Lord
for all his benefits toward me?
I will take the cup of salvation,
and call on the name of the Lord.
I will pay my vows to the Lord,
yes, in the presence of all his people.
Precious in the Lord's sight is the death of his saints.
O Lord, truly I am your servant.
I am your servant, the son of your servant girl.
You have freed me from my chains.

I will offer to you the sacrifice of thanksgiving,
and will call on the name of the Lord.
I will pay my vows to the Lord,
yes, in the presence of all his people,
in the courts of the house of the Lord,
in the middle of you, Jerusalem. Alleluia!
— *Psalm 116:12-19*

Cruciform

The Lord Jesus,
on the night in which he was betrayed, took bread.
When he had given thanks, he broke it and said:
"Take, eat. This is my body, which is broken for you.
Do this in memory of me."
In the same way he also took the cup after supper, saying:
"This cup is the new covenant in my blood.
Do this, as often as you drink, in memory of me."
For as often as you eat this bread and drink this cup,
you proclaim the Lord's death until he comes.
— *1 Corinthians 11:23-26*

Weeks

He who eats my flesh and drinks my blood has eternal life,
and I will raise him up at the last day.
— *John 6:54*

Following the seventh bead:
Glory be to the Father, and to the Son,
and to the Holy Spirit.
As it was in the beginning, is now,
and ever shall be, world without end. Amen.

Dimissory

God our Father,
whose Son our Lord Jesus Christ
in a wonderful Sacrament
has left us a memorial of his passion:
grant us so to venerate the sacred mysteries
of his Body and Blood,
that we may ever perceive within ourselves
the fruit of his redemption;
who lives and reigns with you and the Holy Spirit,
one God, for ever and ever.
— The Collect celebrating the Holy Eucharist◊

In the name of the Father, and of the Son,
and of the Holy Spirit. **Amen.**

≈

Harvest Thanksgiving

Cross

In the name of the Father, and of the Son,
and of the Holy Spirit. **Amen.**

When the Lord restored the fortunes of Zion,
then were we like those who dream.
Then was our mouth filled with laughter
and our tongue with shouts of joy.
Then they said among the nations:
"The Lord has done great things for them."
The Lord has done great things for us,
and we are glad indeed.
Restore our fortunes, O Lord,
like the watercourses of the Negev.

Those who sowed with tears
will reap with songs of joy.
Those who go out weeping, carrying the seed,
will come again with joy, shouldering their sheaves.
— *Psalm 126*◊

Invitatory

Come, let us sing to the Lord;
let us shout for joy to the Rock of our salvation.
Let us come before his presence with thanksgiving
and raise a loud shout to him with psalms.
For the Lord is a great God,
and a great King above all gods.
In his hand are the caverns of the earth,
and the heights of the hills are his also.
The sea is his, for he made it,
and his hands have moulded the dry land.
Come, let us bow down, and bend the knee,
and kneel before the Lord our Maker.
For he is our God,
and we are the people of his pasture
and the sheep of his hand.
Oh, that today you would hearken to his voice!
— *Venite, Psalm 95:1-7*◊

Cruciform

Most certainly, I tell you, it was not Moses
who gave you the bread out of heaven,
but my Father gives you the true bread out of heaven.
For the bread of God is that
which comes down out of heaven,
and gives life to the world.
— *John 6:32-33*

Weeks

Behold, I have brought the first of the fruit of the ground,
which you, O Lord, have given me.
— Deuteronomy 26:10

Following the seventh bead:
Glory be to the Father, and to the Son,
and to the Holy Spirit.
As it was in the beginning, is now,
and ever shall be, world without end. Amen.

Dimissory

Almighty and gracious Father,
we give you thanks for the
fruits of the earth in their season
and for the labours of those who harvest them.
Make us, we pray, faithful stewards of your great bounty,
for the provision of our necessities
and the relief of all who are in need,
to the glory of your Name;
through Jesus Christ our Lord,
who lives and reigns with
you and the Holy Spirit,
one God, now and for ever.
— The Collect for Thanksgiving Day$^\diamond$

In the name of the Father, and of the Son,
and of the Holy Spirit. **Amen.**

∿

Cross

In the name of the Father, and of the Son,
and of the Holy Spirit. **Amen.**

"You say that I am a king.
For this reason I have been born,
and for this reason I have come into the world,
that I should testify to the truth.
Everyone who is of the truth listens to my voice."
— *John 18:37*

Invitatory

Be joyful in the Lord, all you lands;
serve the Lord with gladness
and come before his presence with a song.
Know this: the Lord himself is God;
he himself has made us, and we are his;
we are his people and the sheep of his pasture.
Enter his gates with thanksgiving;
go into his courts with praise;
give thanks to him and call upon his Name.
For the Lord is good;
his mercy is everlasting;
and his faithfulness endures from age to age.
— *Jubilate, Psalm 100*$^\lozenge$

Cruciform

I was hungry
and you gave me food.
I was thirsty
and you gave me drink.

I was a stranger
and you took me in.
I was naked
and you clothed me.
I was sick
and you visited me.
I was in prison
and you came to me.
— *Matthew 25:35-36*

Weeks

Come, you blessed of my Father:
inherit the kingdom prepared for you,
prepared from the foundation of the world.
— *Matthew 25:34*[†]

Following the seventh bead:
Glory be to the Father, and to the Son,
and to the Holy Spirit.
As it was in the beginning, is now,
and ever shall be, world without end. Amen.

Dimissory

Behold, he is coming with the clouds,
and every eye will see him,
including those who pierced him.
All the tribes of the earth will mourn over him.
Even so, amen.
"I am the Alpha and the Omega," says the Lord God,
"who is and who was and who is to come, the Almighty."
— *Revelation 1:7-8*

In the name of the Father, and of the Son,
and of the Holy Spirit. **Amen.**

Feasts (Fixed)

THE PRESENTATION: 2ND FEBRUARY

Cross

In the name of the Father, and of the Son,
and of the Holy Spirit. **Amen.**

How lovely are your dwellings, O Lord of hosts!
My soul longs for the courts of the Lord.
My heart and my flesh cry out for the living God.
The sparrow has found a home,
and the swallow a nest for herself.
Blessed are those who dwell in your house.
They are always praising you.
Blessed are those whose strength is in you,
who have set their hearts on a pilgrimage.
Passing through the valley of weeping,
they make it a place of springs.
The autumn rain covers it with blessings.
They go from strength to strength.
— *Psalm 84:1-7*†

Invitatory

Lift up your heads, you gates!
Be lifted up, you everlasting doors,
and the King of glory will come in.
Who is the King of glory?
The Lord, strong and mighty,
The Lord, mighty in battle.
Lift up your heads, you gates.
Lift them up, you everlasting doors,
and the King of glory will come in.
Who is this King of glory?
The Lord of hosts is the King of glory!
— *Psalm 24:7-10*[†]

Cruciform

Simeon said to Mary: "This child is set
for the falling and the rising of many in Israel.
And a sword will pierce your own soul, too."
— *Luke 2:34-35*[†]

Weeks

Behold, I send my messenger,
and he will prepare the way before me;
the messenger, whom you desire:
behold, he comes!
— *Malachi 3:1*

Following the seventh bead:
Glory be to the Father, and to the Son,
and to the Holy Spirit.
As it was in the beginning, is now,
and ever shall be, world without end. Amen.

Dimissory

Lord, now let your servant depart in peace,
according to your word.
For my eyes have seen your salvation,
which you have prepared before the face of all people,
to be a light to lighten the gentiles,
and to be the glory of your people, Israel.
Glory be to the Father, and to the Son,
and to the Holy Spirit.
As it was in the beginning, is now,
and ever shall be, world without end. Amen.
— *Nunc dimittis, Luke 2:29-32*◊†

In the name of the Father, and of the Son,
and of the Holy Spirit. **Amen.**

∾

The Annunciation: 25th March

Cross

In the name of the Father, and of the Son,
and of the Holy Spirit. **Amen.**

Hail Mary, full of grace!
The Lord is with you.
Blessed are you amongst women,
and blessed is the fruit of your womb, Jesus.
Holy Mary, Mother of God,
pray for us sinners,
now and at the hour of our death.

or

Hail Mary, full of grace!
The Lord is with you.
Blessed are you amongst women,
and blessed is the fruit of your womb, Jesus.
The Holy Spirit will come over you;
and the power of the Most High will overshadow you.
Therefore he who is born from you
will be called the Son of God.
— *Ave Maria; Luke 1:35, 42*[†]

Invitatory

Your throne, O God, is forever and ever.
A sceptre of equity is the sceptre of your kingdom.
You have loved righteousness, and hated wickedness.
Therefore God, your God,
has anointed you with the oil of gladness.
Listen, daughter, and turn your ear.
Forget your own people, and also your father's house.
So the king will desire your beauty,
honour him, for he is your lord.
The daughter of Tyre comes with a gift.
Her clothing is woven with gold.
She shall be led to the king in embroidered work.
Her companions shall be brought to you.
With gladness and rejoicing they shall be led.
They shall enter into the king's palace.
Your sons will take the place of your fathers.
You shall make them princes in all the earth.
I will make your name to be remembered in all generations.
Therefore the peoples shall give you thanks forever and ever.
— *Psalm 45:6-7, 10-17*[†]

Cruciform

The angel said, "Be not afraid, Mary,
for you have found favour with God.

Behold, you will conceive in your womb and give birth to a son,
and shall name him 'Jesus'.
He will be great and will be called the Son of the Most High.
The Lord God will give him the throne of his father David,
and he will reign over the house of Jacob forever,
and of his Kingdom, there shall be no end."
— *Luke 1:30-33*†

Weeks

"Behold, the servant of the Lord;
let it be done to me according to your word."
— *Luke 1:38*

Following the seventh bead:
Glory be to the Father, and to the Son,
and to the Holy Spirit.
As it was in the beginning, is now,
and ever shall be, world without end. Amen.

Dimissory

Our Father,
who art in heaven,
hallowed be thy name.
Thy kingdom come;
thy will be done
on earth as it is in heaven.
Give us this day our daily bread,
and forgive us our trespasses
as we forgive those who trespass against us.
And lead us not into temptation,
but deliver us from evil.
For thine is the kingdom,
and the power, and the glory,
for ever and ever. Amen.

In the name of the Father, and of the Son,
and of the Holy Spirit. **Amen.**

THE VISITATION: 31ST MAY

Cross

In the name of the Father, and of the Son,
and of the Holy Spirit. **Amen.**

Hail Mary, full of grace!
The Lord is with you.
Blessed are you amongst women,
and blessed is the fruit of your womb, Jesus.
Holy Mary, Mother of God,
pray for us sinners,
now and at the hour of our death.

or

Hail Mary, full of grace!
The Lord is with you.
Blessed are you amongst women,
and blessed is the fruit of your womb, Jesus.
The Holy Spirit will come over you;
and the power of the Most High will overshadow you.
Therefore he who is born from you
will be called the Son of God.
— *Ave Maria; Luke 1:35, 42*[†]

Invitatory

Seek the Lord while he wills to be found;
call upon him when he draws near.

Let the wicked forsake their ways
and the evil ones their thoughts.
And let them turn to the Lord, and he will have compassion,
and to our God, for he will richly pardon.
For my thoughts are not your thoughts,
nor your ways my ways, says the Lord.
For as the heavens are higher than the earth,
so are my ways higher than your ways,
and my thoughts than your thoughts.
For as rain and snow fall from the heavens
and return not again, but water the earth,
bringing forth life and giving growth,
seed for sowing and bread for eating,
so is my word that goes forth from my mouth;
it will not return to me empty;
but it will accomplish that which I have purposed,
and prosper in that for which I sent it.
— *Quaerite Dominum, Isaiah 55:6-11*[◊]

Cruciform

The Lord your God is among you,
a mighty one who will save.
He will rejoice over you with joy.
He will calm you in his love.
He will rejoice over you with singing.
— *Zephaniah 3:17*

Weeks

"Blessed is she who believed,
for there will be a fulfilment of the things
which the Lord has spoken!"
— *Luke 1:45*[†]

Following the seventh bead:
Glory be to the Father, and to the Son,
and to the Holy Spirit.
As it was in the beginning, is now,
and ever shall be, world without end. Amen.

Dimissory

My soul proclaims the greatness of the Lord,
and my spirit rejoices in God my Saviour;
for he has looked with favour on his lowly servant;
from this day all generations will call me blessed.
The Almighty has done great things for me,
and holy is his Name.
He has mercy on those who fear him
throughout all generations.
He has shown the strength of his arm;
he has scattered the proud in the imagination of their hearts.
He has cast down the mighty from their thrones,
and has lifted up the humble and meek.
He has filled the hungry with good things,
and the rich he has sent empty away.
He has come to the help of his servant Israel,
for he has remembered his promise of mercy:
the promise he made to our forebears,
to Abraham and his seed for ever.
— *Magnificat, Luke 1:46-55*[◊†]

In the name of the Father, and of the Son,
and of the Holy Spirit. **Amen.**

Cross

In the name of the Father, and of the Son,
and of the Holy Spirit. **Amen.**

It is God who said, "Light will shine out of darkness",
who has shone in our hearts
to give us the light of God's glory,
known in the face of Christ.
— *2 Corinthians 4:6*†

Invitatory

Arise, shine, for your light has come,
and the glory of the Lord has dawned upon you.
For behold, darkness covers the land;
deep gloom enshrouds the peoples.
But over you the Lord will rise,
and his glory will appear upon you.
Nations will stream to your light,
and kings to the brightness of your dawning.
Your gates will always be open;
by day or night they will never be shut.
They will call you, the City of the Lord,
the Zion of the Holy One of Israel.
Violence will no more be heard in your land,
ruin or destruction within your borders.
You will call your walls, Salvation,
and all your portals, Praise.
The sun will no more be your light by day;
by night you will not need the brightness of the moon.
The Lord will be your everlasting light,
and your God will be your glory.
— *Surge illuminare, Isaiah 60:1-3, 11, 14, 18-19*◊

Cruciform

Christ received from God the Father honour and glory
when the voice came to him from the majestic glory.
We heard this voice come out of heaven
when we were with him on the holy mountain.
— *2 Peter 1:17-18*

Weeks

"This is my beloved Son,
in whom I am well pleased.
Listen to him."
— *Matthew 17:5*

Following the seventh bead:
Glory be to the Father, and to the Son,
and to the Holy Spirit.
As it was in the beginning, is now,
and ever shall be, world without end. Amen.

Dimissory

The Lord said to me, "You are my son.
Today I have become your father.
Ask of me, and I will give the nations for your inheritance,
the uttermost parts of the earth for your possession."
Now therefore be wise, you kings.
Be instructed, you judges of the earth.
Serve the Lord with fear, and rejoice with trembling.
Blessed are all those who take refuge in him.
— *Psalm 2:7-8, 10-12*

In the name of the Father, and of the Son,
and of the Holy Spirit. **Amen.**

The Dormition or Assumption of the Blessed Virgin Mary: 15th August

Cross

In the name of the Father, and of the Son,
and of the Holy Spirit. **Amen.**

My soul proclaims the greatness of the Lord,
and my spirit rejoices in God my Saviour;
for he has looked with favour on his lowly servant;
from this day all generations will call me blessed.
The Almighty has done great things for me,
and holy is his Name.
He has mercy on those who fear him
throughout all generations.
He has shown the strength of his arm;
he has scattered the proud in the imagination of their hearts.
He has cast down the mighty from their thrones,
and has lifted up the humble and meek.
He has filled the hungry with good things,
and the rich he has sent empty away.
He has come to the help of his servant Israel,
for he has remembered his promise of mercy:
the promise he made to our forebears,
to Abraham and his seed for ever.
— *Magnificat, Luke 1:46-55*$^{\Diamond\dagger}$

Invitatory

Be joyful in the Lord, all you lands;
serve the Lord with gladness
and come before his presence with a song.

Know this: the Lord himself is God;
he himself has made us, and we are his;
we are his people and the sheep of his pasture.
Enter his gates with thanksgiving;
go into his courts with praise;
give thanks to him and call upon his Name.
For the Lord is good;
his mercy is everlasting;
and his faithfulness endures from age to age.
— *Jubilate, Psalm 100*◊

Cruciform

A great sign was seen in heaven:
a woman clothed with the sun,
and the moon under her feet,
and on her head a crown of twelve stars.
And she gave birth to a son,
who is to rule all the nations.
And I heard a loud voice saying:
"Now the salvation, the power, and the Kingdom of our God,
and the authority of his Christ has come."
— *Revelation 12:1, 5, 10*

Weeks

Hail Mary, full of grace!
The Lord is with you.
Blessed are you amongst women,
and blessed is the fruit of your womb, Jesus.
Holy Mary, Mother of God,
pray for us sinners,
now and at the hour of our death.

or

Hail Mary, full of grace!
The Lord is with you.
Blessed are you amongst women,
and blessed is the fruit of your womb, Jesus.
The Holy Spirit will come over you;
and the power of the Most High will overshadow you.
Therefore he who is born from you
will be called the Son of God.
— *Ave Maria; Luke 1:35, 42*[†]

Following the seventh bead:
Glory be to the Father, and to the Son,
and to the Holy Spirit.
As it was in the beginning, is now,
and ever shall be, world without end. Amen.

Dimissory

O God,
you have taken to yourself the blessed Virgin Mary,
mother of your incarnate Son:
grant that we, who have been redeemed by his blood,
may share with her the glory of your eternal kingdom;
through Jesus Christ our Lord,
who lives and reigns with you,
in the unity of the Holy Spirit,
one God, now and for ever.
— *The Collect for Saint Mary the Virgin*[◊]

In the name of the Father, and of the Son,
and of the Holy Spirit. **Amen.**

∾

Cross

In the name of the Father, and of the Son,
and of the Holy Spirit. **Amen.**

For God so loved the world,
that he gave his only begotten Son,
that whosoever believes in him should not perish,
but have eternal life.
For God sent not his Son into the world to condemn the world,
but that the world through him might be saved.
— *John 3:16-17*[‡†]

Invitatory

Be not far off, O Lord.
You are my help. Hurry to help me!
Deliver my soul from the sword,
my precious life from the power of the dog.
Save me from the lion's mouth!
Yes, you have rescued me from the horns of the wild oxen.
I will declare your name to my brothers.
Among the assembly, I will praise you.
You who fear the Lord, praise him!
All you descendants of Jacob, glorify him!
Stand in awe of him, all you descendants of Israel!
For he has not despised nor abhorred
the affliction of the afflicted,
neither has he hidden his face from him;
but when he cried to him, he heard.
My praise of you comes in the great assembly.
I will pay my vows before those who fear him.

The humble shall eat and be satisfied.
They shall praise the Lord who seek after him.
Let your hearts live forever.
— *Psalm 22:19-26*

Cruciform

Christ,
being in the form of God,
did not consider equality with God a thing to be grasped,
but emptied himself,
taking the form of a servant,
being made in the likeness of men.
And being found in human form,
he humbled himself,
becoming obedient to the point of death,
yes, the death of the cross.
— *Philippians 2:6-11*

Weeks

We adore you, O Christ, and we bless you,
because by your Holy Cross,
you have redeemed the world.
— *The Stations of the Cross*

Following the seventh bead:
Glory be to the Father, and to the Son,
and to the Holy Spirit.
As it was in the beginning, is now,
and ever shall be, world without end. Amen.

Dimissory

Almighty God,
whose Son our Saviour Jesus Christ

was lifted high upon the cross
that he might draw the whole world to himself:
mercifully grant that we,
who glory in the mystery of our redemption,
may have grace to take up our cross and follow him;
who lives and reigns with you
and the Holy Spirit, one God,
in glory everlasting.
— *The Collect for the Holy Cross*[◊]

In the name of the Father, and of the Son,
and of the Holy Spirit. **Amen.**

~

Cross

In the name of the Father, and of the Son,
and of the Holy Spirit. **Amen.**

See how great a love the Father has given to us,
that we should be called children of God!
For this cause the world does not know us,
because it did not know him.
Beloved, now we are children of God.
It is not yet revealed what we will be;
but we know that when he is revealed,
we will be like him; for we will see him just as he is.
— *1 John 3:1-2*

Invitatory

In this mountain, the Lord of hosts will make for all peoples
a feast of choice meat, a feast of choice wines,

of choice meat full of marrow,
of refined choice wines.
He will destroy in this mountain
the covering that hides all peoples,
and the veil that is spread over all nations.
He has swallowed up death forever!
The Lord God will wipe away tears from all faces;
and the reproach of his people
he will take away from all the earth,
for the Lord has spoken it.
It shall be said in that day,
"Behold, this is our God!
We have waited for him, and he will save us!
This is the Lord! We have waited for him.
We will be glad and rejoice in his salvation!"
— *Isaiah 25:6-9*[†]

Cruciform

Blessed be the God and Father of our Lord Jesus Christ,
who by his great mercy caused us to be born again
to a living hope
through the resurrection of Jesus Christ from the dead.
— *1 Peter 1:3*

Weeks

The steadfast love of the Lord never ceases,
his mercies never come to an end;
they are new every morning;
great is your faithfulness.
— *Lamentations 3:22-23, NRSV*

Following the seventh bead:
Glory be to the Father, and to the Son,
and to the Holy Spirit.

As it was in the beginning, is now,
and ever shall be, world without end. Amen.

Dimissory

I saw a new heaven and a new earth:
for the first heaven and the first earth have passed away,
and the sea is no more.
I saw the holy city, New Jerusalem,
coming down out of heaven from God,
prepared like a bride adorned for her husband.
I heard a loud voice out of heaven saying,
"Behold, God's dwelling is with people,
and he will dwell with them, and they will be his people,
and God himself will be with them as their God.
He will wipe away every tear from their eyes.
Death will be no more;
neither will there be mourning, nor crying, nor pain.
The first things have passed away.
I am the Alpha and the Omega,
the Beginning and the End.
I will give freely to him who is thirsty
from the spring of the water of life.
Those who conquer will inherit these things,
and I will be their God, and they will be my people."
— *Revelation 21:1-4, 6; v. 7, NRSV*

In the name of the Father, and of the Son,
and of the Holy Spirit. **Amen.**

Intentions & Intercessions

Cross

In the name of the Father, and of the Son,
and of the Holy Spirit. **Amen.**

The hour comes, and is now,
when the true worshipers
will worship the Father in spirit and truth,
for such the Father seeks to be his worshipers.
God is spirit, and those who worship him
must worship in spirit and truth.
— *John 4:23-24*[†]

Invitatory

Come, Holy Ghost, our souls inspire
and lighten with celestial fire;
thou the anointing Spirit art,
who dost thy sevenfold gifts impart.

Thy blessed unction from above
is comfort, life, and fire of love;
enable with perpetual light
the dullness of our mortal sight.
Teach us to know the Father, Son,
and thee, of both, to be but one;
that through the ages all along
this may be our endless song:
Praise to thine eternal merit,
Father, Son and Holy Spirit. Amen.
— *Veni Creator Spiritus (trans. John Cosin, 1627)*

Cruciform

You will receive power when the Holy Spirit has come upon you.
You will be witnesses to me in Jerusalem,
in all Judea and Samaria,
and to the uttermost parts of the earth.
— *Acts 1:8*

Weeks

As the Father has sent me, even so I send you.
Receive the Holy Spirit.
— *John 20:21-22*

Following the seventh bead:
Glory be to the Father, and to the Son,
and to the Holy Spirit.
As it was in the beginning, is now,
and ever shall be, world without end. Amen.

Dimissory

Arise, shine, for your light has come,
and the glory of the Lord has dawned upon you.

For behold, darkness covers the land;
deep gloom enshrouds the peoples.
But over you the Lord will rise,
and his glory will appear upon you.
Nations will stream to your light,
and kings to the brightness of your dawning.
Your gates will always be open;
by day or night they will never be shut.
They will call you, the City of the Lord,
the Zion of the Holy One of Israel.
Violence will no more be heard in your land,
ruin or destruction within your borders.
You will call your walls, Salvation,
and all your portals, Praise.
The sun will no more be your light by day;
by night you will not need the brightness of the moon.
The Lord will be your everlasting light,
and your God will be your glory.
— *Surge illuminare, Isaiah 60:1-3, 11, 14, 18-19*◊

In the name of the Father, and of the Son,
and of the Holy Spirit. **Amen.**

∼

Gratitude & Thanksgiving

Cross

In the name of the Father, and of the Son,
and of the Holy Spirit. **Amen.**

I am still confident of this:
**I will see the goodness of the Lord
in the land of the living.**
— *Psalm 27:13*

Invitatory

Be joyful in the Lord, all you lands;
serve the Lord with gladness
and come before his presence with a song.
Know this: the Lord himself is God;
he himself has made us, and we are his;
we are his people and the sheep of his pasture.
Enter his gates with thanksgiving;
go into his courts with praise;
give thanks to him and call upon his Name.
For the Lord is good;
his mercy is everlasting;
and his faithfulness endures from age to age.
— *Jubilate, Psalm 100*◊

Cruciform

You are no longer strangers and sojourners,
but fellow citizens with the saints
and members of the household of God.
— *Ephesians 2:19*◊

Weeks

Give thanks to the Lord, for he is good;
for his loving kindness endures forever.
— *Psalm 136:1*

Following the seventh bead:
Glory be to the Father, and to the Son,
and to the Holy Spirit.
As it was in the beginning, is now,
and ever shall be, world without end. Amen.

Dimissory

Rejoice always.
Pray without ceasing.
In everything give thanks,
for this is the will of God in Christ Jesus.
Test all things,
and hold firmly that which is good.
And may the God of peace himself sanctify you in all things.
May your whole spirit, soul, and body
be preserved blameless at the coming of our Lord Jesus Christ.
— *1 Thessalonians 5:16-18, 20, 23*

In the name of the Father, and of the Son,
and of the Holy Spirit. **Amen.**

~

HEALING

Cross

In the name of the Father, and of the Son,
and of the Holy Spirit. **Amen.**

My soul rests in God alone.
My salvation is from him.
He alone is my rock, my salvation, and my fortress.
I will never be greatly shaken.
— *Psalm 62:1-2*

Invitatory

Have you not known?
Have you not heard?

The everlasting God, the Lord,
the Creator of the ends of the earth,
does not faint.
He is not weary.
His understanding is unsearchable.
He gives power to the weak.
He increases the strength of him who has no might.
Those who wait for the Lord will renew their strength.
— *Isaiah 40:28-29, 31*[†]

Cruciform

Come unto me,
all you who travail and are heavy laden,
and I will give you rest.
— *Matthew 11:28*[◊†]

Weeks

The Lord heals the broken in heart,
and binds up their wounds.
— *Psalm 147:3*

Following the seventh bead:
Glory be to the Father, and to the Son,
and to the Holy Spirit.
As it was in the beginning, is now,
and ever shall be, world without end. Amen.

Dimissory

Lord, now let your servant depart in peace,
according to your word.
For my eyes have seen your salvation,
which you have prepared before the face of all people,

to be a light to lighten the gentiles,
and to be the glory of your people, Israel.
— *Nunc dimittis, Luke 2:29-32*^{◊†}

or

Into your hands, O Lord, I commend my spirit;
for you have redeemed me, O Lord, O God of truth.
Keep me, O Lord, as the apple of your eye;
hide me under the shadow of your wings.
— *Compline*^{◊†}

In the name of the Father, and of the Son,
and of the Holy Spirit. **Amen.**

≈

Cross

In the name of the Father, and of the Son,
and of the Holy Spirit. **Amen.**

God be in my head,
and in my understanding;
God be in my eyes,
and in my looking;
God be in my mouth,
and in my speaking;
God be in my heart,
and in my thinking;
God be at my end,
and at my departing.
— *The Sarum Prayer*

Invitatory

See how great a love the Father has given to us,
that we should be called children of God!
For this cause the world does not know us,
because it did not know him.
Beloved, now we are children of God.
It is not yet revealed what we will be;
but we know that when he is revealed,
we will be like him; for we will see him just as he is.
— *1 John 3:1-2*

Cruciform

I have set the Lord always before me.
Because he is at my right hand, I shall not be moved.
Therefore my heart is glad, and my tongue rejoices.
My body shall also dwell in safety.
— *Psalm 16:8-9*

Weeks

Come, O blessed of my Father;
inherit the kingdom prepared for you.
— *Matthew 25:34*$^\diamond$

or

Well done, you good and faithful servant.
Enter into the joy of your lord.
— *Matthew 25:23*†

or

Into paradise may the angels lead you.
At your coming may the martyrs receive you,
and bring you into the holy city Jerusalem.
— *Burial II*$^\lozenge$

or

The Sun of Righteousness is gloriously risen,
giving light to those who sat in darkness
and in the shadow of death.
— *Burial II*$^\lozenge$, *cf. Malachi 4:2, Luke 1:79*

or

The Lord will guide our feet into the way of peace,
having taken away the sin of the world.
— *Burial II*$^\lozenge$, *cf. Luke 1:79*

Following the seventh bead:
Glory be to the Father, and to the Son,
and to the Holy Spirit.
As it was in the beginning, is now,
and ever shall be, world without end. Amen.

Dimissory

Lord, now let your servant depart in peace,
according to your word.
For my eyes have seen your salvation,
which you have prepared before the face of all people,
to be a light to lighten the gentiles,
and to be the glory of your people, Israel.
— *Nunc dimittis, Luke 2:29-32*$^{\lozenge\dagger}$

In the name of the Father, and of the Son,
and of the Holy Spirit. **Amen.**

~

Cross

In the name of the Father, and of the Son,
and of the Holy Spirit. **Amen.**

Our help is in the name of the Lord,
the maker of heaven and earth.
— *Compline*◊

Invitatory

I will lift up my eyes to the hills.
From where does my help come?
My help comes from the Lord,
who made heaven and earth.
He will not let your foot be moved.
He who keeps you will not slumber.
Behold, he who keeps Israel
will neither slumber nor sleep.
The Lord is your keeper.
The Lord is your shade on your right hand.
The sun will not strike you by day,
nor the moon by night.
The Lord will keep you from all evil.
He will keep your soul.
The Lord will keep your going out and your coming in,
from this time forth, and forever more.
— *Psalm 121*†

Cruciform

Into your hands, O Lord, I commend my spirit;
for you have redeemed me, O Lord, O God of truth.
Keep me, O Lord, as the apple of your eye;
hide me under the shadow of your wings.
— *Compline*◊†

Weeks

The Lord is my strength and my shield.
My heart trusts in him, and I am helped.
— *Psalm 28:7*†

Following the seventh bead:
Glory be to the Father, and to the Son,
and to the Holy Spirit.
As it was in the beginning, is now,
and ever shall be, world without end. Amen.

Dimissory

Keep watch, dear Lord,
with those who work, or watch, or weep this night,
and give your angels charge over those who sleep.
Tend the sick, Lord Christ;
give rest to the weary,
bless the dying,
soothe the suffering,
pity the afflicted,
shield the joyous;
and all for your love's sake. Amen.
— *Evening Prayer II*◊

In the name of the Father, and of the Son,
and of the Holy Spirit. **Amen.**

Cross

In the name of the Father, and of the Son,
and of the Holy Spirit. **Amen.**

Our Father,
who art in heaven,
hallowed be thy name.
Thy kingdom come;
thy will be done
on earth as it is in heaven.
Give us this day our daily bread,
and forgive us our trespasses
as we forgive those who trespass against us.
And lead us not into temptation,
but deliver us from evil.
For thine is the kingdom,
and the power, and the glory,
for ever and ever. Amen.

Invitatory

If I say, "Surely the darkness will cover me,
and the light around me turn to night,"
darkness is not dark to you, O Lord;
the night is as bright as the day;
darkness and light to you are both alike.
— *Psalm 139:10-11*$^{\Diamond}$

121

Cruciform

God grant me the serenity
to accept the things I cannot change,
the courage to change the things I can,
and the wisdom to know the difference.
— *The Serenity Prayer*

Weeks

Be still,
and know that I am God.
— *Psalm 46:10*

Following the seventh bead:
Glory be to the Father, and to the Son,
and to the Holy Spirit.
As it was in the beginning, is now,
and ever shall be, world without end. Amen.

Dimissory

Now says the Lord who created you, Jacob,
and he who formed you, Israel:
"Do not be afraid, for I have redeemed you.
I have called you by your name. You are mine.
When you pass through the waters, I will be with you,
and through the rivers, they will not overflow you.
When you walk through the fire, you will not be burned,
and flame will not scorch you.
For I am the Lord your God,
the Holy One of Israel, your Saviour."
— *Isaiah 43:1-3*

In the name of the Father, and of the Son,
and of the Holy Spirit. **Amen.**

Cross

In the name of the Father, and of the Son,
and of the Holy Spirit. **Amen.**

When the Lord restored the fortunes of Zion,
then were we like those who dream.
Then was our mouth filled with laughter
and our tongue with shouts of joy.
Then they said among the nations:
"The Lord has done great things for them."
The Lord has done great things for us,
and we are glad indeed.
Restore our fortunes, O Lord,
like the watercourses of the Negev.
Those who sowed with tears
will reap with songs of joy.
Those who go out weeping, carrying the seed,
will come again with joy, shouldering their sheaves.
— *Psalm 126*[◊]

Invitatory

Blessed are the poor in spirit,
for theirs is the kingdom of heaven.
Blessed are those who mourn,
for they shall be comforted.
Blessed are the gentle,
for they shall inherit the earth.
Blessed are those who hunger and thirst
for righteousness,
for they shall be filled.

Blessed are the merciful,
for they shall obtain mercy.
Blessed are the poor in heart,
for they shall see God.
Blessed are the peacemakers,
for they shall be called children of God.
— *Matthew 5:3-9*

Cruciform

They will beat their swords into ploughshares,
and their spears into pruning hooks.
Nation will not lift up sword against nation,
neither will they learn war any more.
But they will sit every man under his vine and under his fig tree;
and no one will make them afraid.
— *Micah 4:3-4*

Weeks

Jesus came and stood in the middle, saying,
"Peace be with you."
— *John 20:19*[†]

Following the seventh bead:
Glory be to the Father, and to the Son,
and to the Holy Spirit.
As it was in the beginning, is now,
and ever shall be, world without end. Amen.

Dimissory

Then, when he had said this, he breathed on them,
and said to them, "Receive the Holy Spirit!

If you forgive the sins of any,
they have been forgiven them."
— *John 20:22*†

In the name of the Father, and of the Son,
and of the Holy Spirit. **Amen.**

THE PRAYER OF ST. FRANCIS

Cross

In the name of the Father, and of the Son,
and of the Holy Spirit. **Amen.**

Let my prayer be set forth in your sight as incense,
the lifting up of my hands as the evening sacrifice.
—*Psalm 141:2*◊

O God, make speed to save us.
O Lord, make haste to help us.
— *Evening Prayer II*◊

Invitatory

May the words of my mouth,
and the meditation of my heart,
be always acceptable in thy sight, O Lord,
my strength, and my redeemer.
— *Psalm 19:14*‡†

Cruciform

Lord, make me a channel of your peace,
that where there is hatred, I may bring love.

Lord, make me a channel of your peace,
that I may seek to comfort, rather than to be comforted.
Lord, make me a channel of your peace,
that I may seek to understand, rather than to be understood.
— *attributed to St. Francis of Assisi*

.

Weeks

Pray these prayers in order, one for each bead.

Lord, make me a channel of your peace,

1. **that where there is wrong, I may bring forgiveness;**
2. **that where there is discord, I may bring harmony;**
3. **that where there is error, I may bring truth;**
4. **that where there is doubt, I may bring faith;**
5. **that where there is despair, I may bring hope;**
6. **that where there are shadows, I may bring light;**
7. **that where there is sadness, I may bring joy.**
— *attributed to St. Francis of Assisi*

Dimissory

Lord, make me a channel of your peace,
that I may seek to love, rather than to be loved.
For it is by self-forgetting that one finds.
It is by forgiving that one is forgiven.
It is by dying that one awakens to eternal life.
Lord, make me a channel of your peace.
— *attributed to St. Francis of Assisi*

In the name of the Father, and of the Son,
and of the Holy Spirit. **Amen.**

≈

For solo prayer, "we / us" may be changed to "I / me" in the opening confession and the concluding prayer for absolution.

Cross

In the name of the Father, and of the Son,
and of the Holy Spirit. **Amen.**

Rend your hearts and not your garments,
and turn to the Lord, your God;
for he is gracious and merciful,
slow to anger, and abundant in loving kindness.
and relents from sending calamity.
— *Joel 2:13a◊, v. 13b*＊

Invitatory

Most merciful God,
we confess that we have sinned against you
in thought, word, and deed,
by what we have done,
and by what we have left undone.
We have not loved you with our whole heart;
we have not loved our neighbours as ourselves.
We are truly sorry and we humbly repent.
For the sake of your Son Jesus Christ,
have mercy on us and forgive us;
that we may delight in your will,
and walk in your ways,
to the glory of your Name. Amen.
— *Morning Prayer II & Evening Prayer II◊*

or

O Lamb of God, who takes away the sins of the world:
have mercy upon us.
O Lamb of God, who takes away the sins of the world:
have mercy upon us.
O Lamb of God, who takes away the sins of the world:
grant us your peace.
— *Agnus Dei*◊†

Cruciform

Hide your face from my sins,
and blot out all my iniquities.
Create in me a clean heart, O God;
and renew a right spirit within me.
Cast me not away from your presence;
and take not your holy spirit from me.
Restore unto me the joy of your salvation;
and uphold me with a willing spirit.
Then will I teach transgressors your ways;
and sinners shall be converted unto you.
O Lord, open my lips;
and my mouth shall show forth your praise.
— *Psalm 51:9-13, 15*※†

Weeks

Seek first the Kingdom of God and his righteousness;
and all these things shall be added unto you.
— *Matthew 6:33*※†

Following the seventh bead:
Glory be to the Father, and to the Son,
and to the Holy Spirit.
As it was in the beginning, is now,
and ever shall be, world without end. Amen.

Dimissory

May almighty God have mercy on us, forgive us all our sins
through our Lord Jesus Christ, strengthen us in all goodness, and
by the power of the Holy Spirit keep us in eternal life. **Amen.**
— *Morning Prayer II & Evening Prayer II*^{◊†}

God, being rich in mercy,
for his great love with which he loved us,
even when we were dead through our trespasses,
made us alive together with Christ —
by grace you have been saved —
and raised us up with him,
and made us to sit with him
in the heavenly places in Christ Jesus.
— *Ephesians 2:4-6*

In the name of the Father, and of the Son,
and of the Holy Spirit. **Amen.**

≈

Vocation & Dedication of Self

Cross

In the name of the Father, and of the Son,
and of the Holy Spirit. **Amen.**

Peace be with you. As the Father has sent me,
even so I send you. Receive the Holy Spirit!
— *John 20:21-22*[†]

Invitatory

Now says the Lord who created you, Jacob,
and he who formed you, Israel:
"Do not be afraid, for I have redeemed you.
I have called you by your name. You are mine.
When you pass through the waters, I will be with you,
and through the rivers, they will not overflow you.
When you walk through the fire, you will not be burned,
and flame will not scorch you.
For I am the Lord your God,
the Holy One of Israel, your Saviour."
— *Isaiah 43:1-3*

Cruciform

You did not choose me,
but I chose you.
And I appointed you to go and bear fruit,
fruit that will last.
— *John 15:16, NRSV*

Weeks

Here am I;
send me.
— *Isaiah 6:8*[※]

Following the seventh bead:
Glory be to the Father, and to the Son,
and to the Holy Spirit.
As it was in the beginning, is now,
and ever shall be, world without end. Amen.

Dimissory

"I know the thoughts that I think toward you," says the Lord,
"thoughts of peace, and not of evil,
to give you hope and a future.
You shall call on me,
and you shall go and pray to me,
and I will listen to you.
You shall seek me, and find me,
when you search for me with all your heart.
I will be found by you," says the Lord.
— *Jeremiah 29:11-14*

In the name of the Father, and of the Son,
and of the Holy Spirit. **Amen.**

WISDOM

Cross

In the name of the Father, and of the Son,
and of the Holy Spirit. **Amen.**

Does not wisdom cry out?
Does not understanding raise her voice?
"The Lord possessed me in the beginning of his work,
before his deeds of old.
I was set up from everlasting, from the beginning,
before the earth existed.
When there were no depths, I was born,
when there were no springs abounding with water.
Before the mountains were settled in place,
before the hills, I was born;

while as yet he had not made the earth, nor the fields,
nor the beginning of the dust of the world."
— *Proverbs 8:1, 22-26*

Invitatory

Blessed be the name of God forever and ever;
for wisdom and might are his.
He changes the times and the seasons.
He removes kings and sets up kings.
He gives wisdom to the wise,
and knowledge to those who have understanding.
He reveals the deep and secret things.
He knows what is in the darkness,
and the light dwells with him.
I thank you and praise you, O God of my fathers,
who have given me wisdom and might.
— *Daniel 2:20-23*

Cruciform

If any of you lacks wisdom,
let him ask of God,
who gives to all liberally and without reproach.
But let him ask in faith,
without any doubting,
and be doers of the word,
not only hearers.
— *James 1:5-6, 22*[†]

Weeks

Seek first the Kingdom of God and his righteousness;
and all these things shall be added unto you.
— *Matthew 6:33*[*][†]

Following the seventh bead:
Glory be to the Father, and to the Son,
and to the Holy Spirit.
**As it was in the beginning, is now,
and ever shall be, world without end. Amen.**

Dimissory

Does not wisdom cry out?
Does not understanding raise her voice?
"When the Lord established the heavens, I was there.
When he set a circle on the surface of the deep,
when he established the clouds above,
when the springs of the deep became strong,
when he gave to the sea its boundary,
that the waters should not violate his commandment,
when he marked out the foundations of the earth,
then I was the craftsman by his side.
I was a delight day by day,
always rejoicing before him,
rejoicing in his whole world.
My delight was with the sons of men."
— *Proverbs 8:1, 27-31*

In the name of the Father, and of the Son,
and of the Holy Spirit. **Amen.**

∾

BEATITUDES

Cross

In the name of the Father, and of the Son,
and of the Holy Spirit. **Amen.**

O God, make speed to save us.
O Lord, make haste to help us.
— *Evening Prayer II*◊

Invitatory

If anyone is in Christ he is a new creation;
the old has passed away, behold the new has come.
All this is from God,
who through Christ reconciled us to himself
and gave us the ministry of reconciliation.
— *2 Corinthians 5:17-18*◊

Cruciform

Be merciful, even as your Father is merciful.
Judge not, and you shall not be judged.
Condemn not, and you shall not be condemned.
Set free, and you shall be set free.
— *Luke 6:36-37a**†*, v. 37b**†

Weeks

Pray these prayers in order, one for each bead.

1. Blessed are the poor in spirit,
for theirs is the Kingdom of Heaven.

2. Blessed are those who mourn,
for they shall be comforted.

3. Blessed are the gentle,
for they shall inherit the earth.

4. Blessed are those who hunger and thirst for righteousness,
for they shall be filled.

5. Blessed are the merciful,
for they shall obtain mercy.

6. Blessed are the poor in heart,
for they shall see God.

7. Blessed are the peacemakers,
for they shall be called children of God.
— *Matthew 5:3-9*

Following the seventh bead:
Glory be to the Father, and to the Son,
and to the Holy Spirit.
As it was in the beginning, is now,
and ever shall be, world without end. Amen.

Dimissory

Blessed are those who have been persecuted
for righteousness' sake,
for theirs is the Kingdom of Heaven.
Blessed are you when people reproach you,
persecute you,
and speak evil of you falsely, for my sake.
Rejoice, and be exceedingly glad,
for great is your reward in heaven.
For that is how they persecuted the prophets before you.
Even so, let your light shine before men,
that they may see your good works
and glorify your Father who is in heaven.
— *Matthew 5:10-12, 16*[†]

In the name of the Father, and of the Son,
and of the Holy Spirit. **Amen.**

∾

Cross

In the name of the Father, and of the Son,
and of the Holy Spirit. **Amen.**

Our Father,
who art in heaven,
hallowed be thy name.
Thy kingdom come;
thy will be done
on earth as it is in heaven.
Give us this day our daily bread,
and forgive us our trespasses
as we forgive those who trespass against us.
And lead us not into temptation,
but deliver us from evil.
For thine is the kingdom,
and the power, and the glory,
for ever and ever. Amen.

Invitatory

For everything there is a season,
and a time for every purpose under heaven:
a time to be born, and a time to die;
a time to plant, and a time to pluck up that which is planted;
a time to kill, and a time to heal;
a time to break down, and a time to build up;
a time to weep, and a time to laugh;
a time to mourn, and a time to dance;
a time to cast away stones,
and a time to gather stones together;
a time to embrace, and a time to refrain from embracing;
a time to seek, and a time to lose;
a time to keep, and a time to cast away;

a time to tear, and a time to sew;
a time to keep silence, and a time to speak;
a time to love, and a time to hate;
a time for war, and a time for peace.
— *Ecclesiastes 3:1-8*

Cruciform

Wait for the promise of the Father,
which you heard from me.
For John indeed baptised in water,
but you will be baptised in the Holy Spirit.
— *Acts 1:4-5*

Weeks

I wait for the Lord.
My soul waits. I hope in his word.
— *Psalm 130:5*

Following the seventh bead:
Glory be to the Father, and to the Son,
and to the Holy Spirit.
As it was in the beginning, is now,
and ever shall be, world without end. Amen.

Dimissory

Blessed be the Lord, the God of Israel;
he has come to his people and set them free.
He has raised up for us a mighty saviour,
born of the house of his servant David.
Through his holy prophets he promised of old,
that he would save us from our enemies,
from the hands of all who hate us.

He promised to show mercy to our fathers
and to remember his holy covenant.
This was the oath he swore to our father Abraham,
to set us free from the hands of our enemies,
free to worship him without fear,
holy and righteous in his sight
all the days of our life.
You, my child, shall be called the prophet of the Most High,
for you will go before the Lord to prepare his way,
to give his people knowledge of salvation
by the forgiveness of their sins.
In the tender compassion of our God
the dawn from on high shall break upon us,
to shine on those who dwell in darkness and the shadow of death,
and to guide our feet into the way of peace.
— *Benedictus Dominus Deus, Luke 1:68-79*[◊]

In the name of the Father, and of the Son,
and of the Holy Spirit. **Amen.**

∼

DOUBT

Cross

In the name of the Father, and of the Son,
and of the Holy Spirit. **Amen.**

Now says the Lord who created you, Jacob,
and he who formed you, Israel:
"Do not be afraid, for I have redeemed you.
I have called you by your name. You are mine.
When you pass through the waters, I will be with you,
and through the rivers, they will not overflow you.
When you walk through the fire, you will not be burned,
and flame will not scorch you.

For I am the Lord your God,
the Holy One of Israel, your Saviour."
— *Isaiah 43:1-3*

Invitatory

The Lord passed by,
and a great and strong wind tore the mountains,
and broke in pieces the rocks before the Lord;
but the Lord was not in the wind.
After the wind there was an earthquake;
but the Lord was not in the earthquake.
After the earthquake a fire passed;
but the Lord was not in the fire.
After the fire, there was a still small voice:
"What are you doing here?"
— *1 Kings 19:11-13*

Cruciform

In the beginning was the Word,
and the Word was with God,
and the Word was God.
In him was life,
and the life was the light of men.
The light shines in the darkness,
and the darkness has not overcome it.
— *John 1:1, 4-5*

Weeks

I believe;
help thou mine unbelief.
— *Mark 9:24*[*]

Glory be to the Father, and to the Son,
and to the Holy Spirit.
As it was in the beginning, is now,
and ever shall be, world without end. Amen.

Dimissory

I arise today, through God's strength to pilot me,
God's might to uphold me,
God's wisdom to guide me,
God's eye to look before me,
God's ear to hear me,
God's word to speak for me,
God's hand to guard me,
God's shield to protect me,
God's host to save me
from snares of devils,
from temptation of vices,
from everyone who shall wish me ill, afar and near.
I summon today all these powers
between me and those evils.
— *St. Patrick's Breastplate*

In the name of the Father, and of the Son,
and of the Holy Spirit. **Amen.**

∾

WEARINESS

Cross

In the name of the Father, and of the Son,
and of the Holy Spirit. **Amen.**

The Lord Jesus Christ says:
"Take my yoke upon you, and learn from me;
for I am gentle and lowly in heart,
and you will find rest for your souls.
For my yoke is easy,
and my burden is light."
— *Matthew 11:29-30*

Invitatory

The Lord is my shepherd:
I shall lack nothing.
He makes me lie down in green pastures.
He leads me beside still waters.
He restores my soul.
He guides me in the paths of righteousness for his name's sake.
Even though I walk through the valley of the shadow of death,
I will fear no evil, for you are with me.
Your rod and your staff,
they comfort me.
You prepare a table before me
in the presence of my enemies.
You anoint my head with oil.
My cup runs over.
Surely goodness and loving kindness
shall follow me all the days of my life,
and I will dwell in the house of the Lord forever.
— *Psalm 23*[†]

Cruciform

Lord, you are in the midst of us,
and we are called by your name:
do not forsake us, O Lord our God.
— *Jeremiah 14:9, 21*[◊]

Weeks

Come unto me,
all you who travail and are heavy laden,
and I will give you rest.
— *Matthew 11:28*[◊†]

Following the seventh bead:
Glory be to the Father, and to the Son,
and to the Holy Spirit.
As it was in the beginning, is now,
and ever shall be, world without end. Amen.

Dimissory

Into your hands, O Lord, I commend my spirit;
for you have redeemed me, O Lord, O God of truth.
Keep me, O Lord, as the apple of your eye;
hide me under the shadow of your wings.
— *Compline*[◊†]

In the name of the Father, and of the Son,
and of the Holy Spirit. **Amen.**

∽

HOPELESSNESS (OR WHEN GOD SEEMS SILENT)

Cross

In the name of the Father, and of the Son,
and of the Holy Spirit. **Amen.**

Because you have made the Lord your refuge,
and the Most High your dwelling place,

no evil shall happen to you,
neither shall any plague come near your dwelling.
For he will put his angels in charge of you,
to guard you in all your ways.
— *Psalm 91:9-11*

or

Out of the depths I have cried to you, O Lord.
Lord, hear my voice.
Let your ears attend to the voice of my petitions.
If you, Lord, kept a record of sins,
Lord, who could stand?
But there is forgiveness with you,
therefore you are feared.
I wait for the Lord.
My soul waits. I hope in his word.
My soul longs for the Lord
more than watchmen long for the morning,
more than watchmen for the morning.
— *Psalm 130:1-6*

Invitatory

My God, my God, why have you forsaken me?
Why are you so far from helping me,
and from the words of my groaning?
My God, I cry in the daytime, but you do not answer;
in the night season, and am not silent.
But you are holy,
you who inhabit the praises of Israel.
Our fathers trusted in you.
They trusted, and you delivered them.
They cried to you, and were delivered.
They trusted in you, and were not disappointed.

Be not far from me, for trouble is near.
For there is no one to help.
— *Psalm 22:1-4, 11*

Cruciform

Be not far off, O Lord.
You are my help. Hurry to help me!
Deliver my soul from the sword,
my precious life from the power of the dog.
— *Psalm 22:19-20*[†]

Weeks

Save us from the time of trial,
and deliver us from evil.

Following the seventh bead:
Glory be to the Father, and to the Son,
and to the Holy Spirit.
As it was in the beginning, is now,
and ever shall be, world without end. Amen.

Dimissory

He who calls you is faithful.
He who calls you is faithful.
— *1 Thessalonians 5:24*

In the name of the Father, and of the Son,
and of the Holy Spirit. **Amen.**

∾

Cross

In the name of the Father, and of the Son,
and of the Holy Spirit. **Amen.**

Let us draw near with boldness to the throne of grace,
that we may receive mercy
and may find grace for help in time of need.
— *Hebrews 4:16*

or

I desire mercy, and not sacrifice;
and the knowledge of God more than burnt offerings.
— *Hosea 6:6‡*

or

O Lamb of God, who takes away the sins of the world:
have mercy upon us.
O Lamb of God, who takes away the sins of the world:
have mercy upon us.
O Lamb of God, who takes away the sins of the world:
grant us your peace.
— *Agnus Dei◊†*

Invitatory

Create in me a clean heart, O God;
and renew a right spirit within me.
Cast me not away from your presence;
and take not your holy spirit from me.
Restore unto me the joy of your salvation;
and uphold me with a willing spirit.
— *Psalm 51:10-12*†

Cruciform

The steadfast love of the Lord never ceases;
his mercies never come to an end.
They are new every morning.
Great is your faithfulness.
— *Lamentations 3:22-23, NRSV*

Weeks

Be merciful,
even as your Father is also merciful.
— *Luke 6:36*

Following the seventh bead:
Glory be to the Father, and to the Son,
and to the Holy Spirit.
**As it was in the beginning, is now,
and ever shall be, world without end. Amen.**

Dimissory

Show us your mercy, O Lord;
and grant us your salvation.
Clothe your ministers with righteousness;
let your people sing with joy.
Give peace, O Lord, in all the world;
for only in you can we live in safety.
Lord, keep this nation under your care;
and guide us in the way of justice and truth.
Let your way be known upon earth;
your saving health among all nations.
Let not the needy, O Lord, be forgotten;
nor the hope of the poor be taken away.

Create in us clean hearts, O God;
and sustain us with your Holy Spirit.
— *Versicles & Responses, Morning Prayer II*◊

In the name of the Father, and of the Son,
and of the Holy Spirit. **Amen.**

FOR A LOVED ONE

Cross

In the name of the Father, and of the Son,
and of the Holy Spirit. **Amen.**

May the words of my mouth,
and the meditation of my heart,
be always acceptable in thy sight, O Lord,
my strength, and my redeemer.
— *Psalm 19:14*‡†

Invitatory

Is any among you suffering?
Let him pray.
Is any cheerful?
Let him sing praises.
Is any among you sick?
Let the elders of the assembly pray over him,
and anoint with oil in the name of the Lord,
and the prayer of faith will heal.
— *James 5:13-15*†

Cruciform

Spend time considering your petition and offering your loved one(s) to God. For group prayer, "my" and "I" may be changed to "our" and "we".

O Lord, my God, I offer into your care
the life of _____, your beloved child(ren).
Grant *him / her / them* light in the darkness.
Be an anchor in the waves.
May your saints and angels surround *him / her / them*.
And may your protection, your love, and your peace abide.

Weeks

Stay with us, Lord,
for you are our life.
— *The Prayer of St. Padre Pio following Communion*[†]

Following the seventh bead:
Glory be to the Father, and to the Son,
and to the Holy Spirit.
As it was in the beginning, is now,
and ever shall be, world without end. Amen.

Dimissory

Lord, now let your servant depart in peace,
according to your word.
For my eyes have seen your salvation,
which you have prepared before the face of all people,
to be a light to lighten the gentiles,
and to be the glory of your people, Israel.
— *Nunc dimittis, Luke 2:29-32*[◊†]

In the name of the Father, and of the Son,
and of the Holy Spirit. **Amen.**

Cross

In the name of the Father, and of the Son,
and of the Holy Spirit. **Amen.**

Now says the Lord who created you, Jacob,
and he who formed you, Israel:
"Do not be afraid, for I have redeemed you.
I have called you by your name. You are mine.
When you pass through the waters, I will be with you,
and through the rivers, they will not overflow you.
When you walk through the fire, you will not be burned,
and flame will not scorch you.
For I am the Lord your God,
the Holy One of Israel, your Saviour."
— *Isaiah 43:1-3*

Invitatory

He who dwells in the secret place of the Most High
will rest in the shadow of the Almighty.
I will say of the Lord, "He is my refuge and my fortress;
my God, in whom I trust."
For he will deliver you from the snare of the fowler,
and from the deadly pestilence.
He will cover you with his feathers.
Under his wings you will take refuge.
His faithfulness is your shield and rampart.
You shall not be afraid of the terror by night,
nor of the arrow that flies by day.

For he will put his angels in charge of you,
to guard you in all your ways.
They will bear you up in their hands,
so that you will not dash your foot against a stone.
You will tread on the lion and cobra.
You will trample the young lion and the serpent underfoot.
"Because he has set his love on me, therefore I will deliver him.
I will set him on high, because he has known my name.
He will call on me, and I will answer him.
I will be with him in trouble.
I will deliver him, and honour him.
I will satisfy him with long life,
and show him my salvation."
— *Psalm 91:1-5, 11-16*

Cruciform

On the night he was betrayed, our Lord Jesus Christ prayed:
"My Father, if it is possible, let this cup pass away from me!
Yet not what I desire, but what you desire."
— *Matthew 26:39*†

Weeks

Pray without ceasing.
He who calls you is faithful.
— *1 Thessalonians 5:17, 24*

Following the seventh bead:
Glory be to the Father, and to the Son,
and to the Holy Spirit.
As it was in the beginning, is now,
and ever shall be, world without end. Amen.

Dimissory

Into your hands, O Lord, I commend my spirit.
Into your hands, O Lord, I commend my spirit.
For you have redeemed me, O Lord, O God of truth.
I commend my spirit.
Keep me, O Lord, as the apple of your eye;
hide me under the shadow of your wings.
Into your hands, O Lord,
I commend my spirit.
— *Compline*◊†

In the name of the Father, and of the Son,
and of the Holy Spirit. **Amen.**

When We Do Not Understand

Cross

In the name of the Father, and of the Son,
and of the Holy Spirit. **Amen.**

In the beginning,
God created the heavens and the earth.
The earth was formless and empty.
Darkness was on the surface of the deep
and God's Spirit was hovering
over the surface of the waters.
God said, "Let there be light,"
and there was light.
God saw the light,
and saw that it was good.
— *Genesis 1:1-4*

Invitatory

Brothers and sisters,
whatever things are true,
whatever things are honourable,
whatever things are just,
whatever things are pure,
whatever things are lovely,
whatever things are of good report:
if there is any virtue and if there is any praise,
think about these things.
— *Philippians 4:8*[†]

Cruciform

Beloved, now we are children of God.
It is not yet revealed what we will be;
but we know that when he is revealed,
we will be like him; for we will see him just as he is.
Everyone who has this hope set on him purifies himself,
even as he is pure.
— *1 John 3:2-3*

or

By this God's love was revealed in us,
that God has sent his one and only Son into the world
that we might live through him.
In this is love,
not that we loved God,
but that he loved us.
— *1 John 4:9-10*

Weeks

My little children, let us not love in word only,
or with the tongue only, but in deed and truth.
— *1 John 3:18*

Following the seventh bead:
Glory be to the Father, and to the Son,
and to the Holy Spirit.
As it was in the beginning, is now,
and ever shall be, world without end. Amen.

Dimissory

God be in my head,
and in my understanding;
God be in my eyes,
and in my looking;
God be in my mouth,
and in my speaking;
God be in my heart,
and in my thinking;
God be at my end,
and at my departing.
— *The Sarum Prayer*

In the name of the Father, and of the Son,
and of the Holy Spirit. **Amen.**

Cross

In the name of the Father, and of the Son,
and of the Holy Spirit. **Amen.**

Our Father,
who art in heaven,
hallowed be thy name.
Thy kingdom come;
thy will be done
on earth as it is in heaven.
Give us this day our daily bread,
and forgive us our trespasses
as we forgive those who trespass against us.
And lead us not into temptation,
but deliver us from evil.
For thine is the kingdom,
and the power, and the glory,
for ever and ever. Amen.

Invitatory

Do not let the sun go down on your wrath,
and do not give place to the devil.
Let no corrupt speech leave your mouth,
but only what builds up, that it may give grace.
Do not grieve the Holy Spirit of God,
in whom you were sealed.
Put away bitterness, wrath, and malice.
Be kind to one another, tender hearted,
forgiving each other,
just as God also in Christ forgave you.
— *Ephesians 4:26, 28-32*

Cruciform

O Lamb of God, who takes away the sins of the world:
have mercy upon us.
O Lamb of God, who takes away the sins of the world:
have mercy upon us.
O Lamb of God, who takes away the sins of the world:
grant us your peace.
— *Agnus Dei*◊†

Weeks

Specific petitions may be thought upon and offered.

Create in me a clean heart, O God;
and renew a right spirit within me.
— *Psalm 51:10*‡

Following the seventh bead:
Glory be to the Father, and to the Son,
and to the Holy Spirit.
As it was in the beginning, is now,
and ever shall be, world without end. Amen.

Dimissory

Come unto me,
all you who travail and are heavy laden,
and I will give you rest.
Take my yoke upon you, and learn from me;
for I am gentle and humble in heart,
and you will find rest for your souls.
For my yoke is easy,
and my burden is light.
— *Matthew 11:28*◊†*; vv. 29-30*✱

In the name of the Father, and of the Son,
and of the Holy Spirit. **Amen.**

Cross

In the name of the Father, and of the Son,
and of the Holy Spirit. **Amen.**

The souls of the righteous are in the hand of God,
and no torment will touch them.
In the eyes of the foolish they seemed to have died.
Their departure was considered a disaster,
and their travel away from us ruin,
but they are in peace.
The Lord will reign over them forever.
Those who trust him will understand truth.
The faithful will live with him in love,
because grace and mercy are with his chosen ones.
— *Wisdom of Solomon 3:1-3, 8-9*

Invitatory

Behold, God's dwelling is with people,
and he will dwell with them,
and they will be his people,
and God himself will be with them.
He will wipe away every tear from their eyes.
Death will be no more;
neither will there be mourning, nor crying, nor pain.
The first things have passed away.
— *Revelation 21:3-4*

Cruciform

For I am persuaded that neither death, nor life,
nor angels, nor principalities,
nor things present, nor things to come,
nor powers,
nor height, nor depth,
nor any other created thing
will be able to separate us from God's love
which is in Christ Jesus our Lord.
— *Romans 8:38-39*

Weeks

At the beginning of each Week, pray the following:

Father of all, we pray to you for _____,
and for all those whom we love and see no longer.
— *Burial II*◊

Then seven times, one per bead, as normal:

Rest eternal grant *him / her / them*, O Lord,
and let light perpetual shine upon *him / her / them*.

Following the seventh bead:
Glory be to the Father, and to the Son,
and to the Holy Spirit.
As it was in the beginning, is now,
and ever shall be, world without end. Amen.

Dimissory

The Lord assigned my portion and my cup.
You made my lot secure.

The lines have fallen to me in pleasant places.
Yes, I have a good inheritance.
I will bless the Lord, who has given me counsel.
Yes, my heart instructs me in the night seasons.
I have set the Lord always before me.
Because he is at my right hand, I shall not be moved.
Therefore my heart is glad, and my tongue rejoices.
My body shall also dwell in safety.
For you will not leave my soul in Sheol,
neither will you allow your holy one to see corruption.
You will show me the path of life.
In your presence is fullness of joy.
In your right hand there are pleasures forever more.
— *Psalm 16:5-11*

Give rest, O Christ, to your servant(s) with your saints,
where sorrow and pain are no more,
neither sighing, but life everlasting.
— *Burial II*[◊]

In the name of the Father, and of the Son,
and of the Holy Spirit. **Amen.**

DECISION MAKING

Cross

In the name of the Father, and of the Son,
and of the Holy Spirit. **Amen.**

If then you have been raised with Christ,
seek the things that are above, where Christ is,
seated at the right hand of God.
— *Colossians 3:1*[◊]

Invitatory

The Lord is my shepherd:
I shall lack nothing.
He makes me lie down in green pastures.
He leads me beside still waters.
He restores my soul.
He guides me in the paths of righteousness for his name's sake.
Even though I walk through the valley of the shadow of death,
I will fear no evil, for you are with me.
Your rod and your staff,
they comfort me.
You prepare a table before me
in the presence of my enemies.
You anoint my head with oil.
My cup runs over.
Surely goodness and loving kindness
shall follow me all the days of my life,
and I will dwell in the house of the Lord forever.
— *Psalm 23*[†]

Cruciform

May the words of my mouth,
and the meditation of my heart,
be always acceptable in thy sight, O Lord,
my strength, and my redeemer.
— *Psalm 19:14*[‡†]

Weeks

At the beginning of each Week, consider or speak your petition.

Send out your light and your truth, that they may lead me,
and bring me to your holy hill and to your dwelling.
— *Psalm 43:3*[◊]

Following the seventh bead:
Glory be to the Father, and to the Son,
and to the Holy Spirit.
As it was in the beginning, is now,
and ever shall be, world without end. Amen.

Dimissory

I will bless the Lord, who has given me counsel.
Yes, my heart instructs me in the night seasons.
I have set the Lord always before me.
Because he is at my right hand, I shall not be moved.
Therefore my heart is glad, and my tongue rejoices.
My body shall also dwell in safety.
— *Psalm 16:7-9*

In the name of the Father, and of the Son,
and of the Holy Spirit. **Amen.**

∾

Cross

In the name of the Father, and of the Son,
and of the Holy Spirit. **Amen.**

When he, the Spirit of truth, has come,
he will guide you into all truth.
He will declare to you things that are coming.
He will glorify me,
for he will take from what is mine,
and will declare it to you.
A little while, and you will not see me.
Again a little while, and you will see me.
— *John 16:13-14, 16*

Invitatory

For everything there is a season,
and a time for every purpose under heaven:
a time to be born, and a time to die;
a time to plant, and a time to pluck up that which is planted;
a time to kill, and a time to heal;
a time to break down, and a time to build up;
a time to weep, and a time to laugh;
a time to mourn, and a time to dance;
a time to cast away stones,
and a time to gather stones together;
a time to embrace, and a time to refrain from embracing;
a time to seek, and a time to lose;
a time to keep, and a time to cast away;
a time to tear, and a time to sew;
a time to keep silence, and a time to speak;
a time to love, and a time to hate;
a time for war, and a time for peace.
— *Ecclesiastes 3:1-8*

Cruciform

Into your hands, O Lord, I commend my spirit;
for you have redeemed me, O Lord, O God of truth.
I trust in you, O Lord. I said, "You are my God."
My times are in your hand.
— *Psalm 31:5, Compline◊, vv. 14-15*

Weeks

At the beginning of each Week, consider or speak your petition.

Your word is a lamp to my feet,
and a light for my path.
— *Psalm 119:105*

Following the seventh bead:
Glory be to the Father, and to the Son,
and to the Holy Spirit.
**As it was in the beginning, is now,
and ever shall be, world without end. Amen.**

Dimissory

May the God of all grace,
who called you to his eternal glory by Christ Jesus,
after you have suffered a little while,
perfect, establish, strengthen, and settle you.
To him be the glory and the power
forever and ever. Amen.
— *1 Peter 5:10-11*

In the name of the Father, and of the Son,
and of the Holy Spirit. **Amen.**

∿

SOCIAL JUSTICE

Cross

In the name of the Father, and of the Son,
and of the Holy Spirit. **Amen.**

Pure religion and undefiled before our God and Father is this:
**to visit the fatherless and widows in their affliction,
and to keep oneself unstained by the world.**
— *James 1:27*

Invitatory

My soul proclaims the greatness of the Lord,
and my spirit rejoices in God my Saviour;
for he has looked with favour on his lowly servant;
from this day all generations will call me blessed.
The Almighty has done great things for me,
and holy is his Name.
He has mercy on those who fear him
throughout all generations.
He has shown the strength of his arm;
he has scattered the proud in the imagination of their hearts.
He has cast down the mighty from their thrones,
and has lifted up the humble and meek.
He has filled the hungry with good things,
and the rich he has sent empty away.
He has come to the help of his servant Israel,
for he has remembered his promise of mercy:
the promise he made to our forebears,
to Abraham and his seed for ever.
— *Magnificat, Luke 1:46-55*^{◊†}

Cruciform

I will give you as a light to the nations,
that my salvation may reach to the end of the earth.
— *Isaiah 49:6*[◊]

Weeks

At the beginning of each Week, consider or speak your petition.

Let justice roll on like rivers,
and righteousness like a mighty stream.
— *Amos 5:24*

Glory be to the Father, and to the Son,
and to the Holy Spirit.
As it was in the beginning, is now,
and ever shall be, world without end. Amen.

Dimissory

The righteous will ask:
"Lord, when did we see you hungry and feed you,
or thirsty and give you a drink?
When did we see you as a stranger and take you in,
or naked and clothe you?
When did we see you sick or in prison
and come to you?"
The King will answer them,
"Most certainly I tell you,
because you did it to one of the least of these my brothers,
you did it to me."
— *Matthew 25:37-40*[†]

In the name of the Father, and of the Son,
and of the Holy Spirit. **Amen.**

THE THINGS WE CANNOT SHARE

Cross

In the name of the Father, and of the Son,
and of the Holy Spirit. **Amen.**

If I say, "Surely the darkness will cover me,
and the light around me turn to night,"

darkness is not dark to you, O Lord;
the night is as bright as the day;
darkness and light to you are both alike.
— *Psalm 139:10-11*◊

Invitatory

I am the light of the world; whoever follows me
will not walk in darkness, but will have the light of life.
— *John 8:12*◊

Do not be afraid, for I have redeemed you.
I have called you by your name. You are mine.
— *Isaiah 43:1*

Cruciform

Our help is in the name of the Lord,
the maker of heaven and earth.
— *Compline*◊

Weeks

Christ be with me,
Christ beside me,
Christ before me,
Christ behind me.
— *St. Patrick's Breastplate*

Following the seventh bead:
Glory be to the Father, and to the Son,
and to the Holy Spirit.
As it was in the beginning, is now,
and ever shall be, world without end. Amen.

Dimissory

Into your hands, O Lord, I commend my spirit;
for you have redeemed me, O Lord, O God of truth.
Keep me, O Lord, as the apple of your eye;
hide me under the shadow of your wings.
— *Compline*◊†

In the name of the Father, and of the Son,
and of the Holy Spirit. **Amen.**

∾

When You Don't Know What to Pray

Cross

In the name of the Father, and of the Son,
and of the Holy Spirit. **Amen.**

Our Father,
who art in heaven,
hallowed be thy name.
Thy kingdom come;
thy will be done
on earth as it is in heaven.
Give us this day our daily bread,
and forgive us our trespasses
as we forgive those who trespass against us.
And lead us not into temptation,
but deliver us from evil.
For thine is the kingdom,
and the power, and the glory,
for ever and ever. Amen.

Invitatory

Let the earth glorify the Lord:
praise him and highly exalt him for ever.
Glorify the Lord, O mountains and hills,
and all that grows upon the earth:
praise him and highly exalt him for ever.
Glorify the Lord, O springs of water, seas, and streams,
O whales and all that move in the waters.
All birds of the air, glorify the Lord:
praise him and highly exalt him for ever.
Glorify the Lord, O beasts of the wild,
and all you flocks and herds.
O men and women everywhere, glorify the Lord:
praise him and highly exalt him for ever.
— *The Song of the Three Young Men 74-82*◊

Cruciform

May the words of my mouth,
and the meditation of my heart,
be always acceptable in thy sight, O Lord,
my strength, and my redeemer.
— *Psalm 19:14*‡†

or

Yours is the day, O God, yours also the night;
you established the moon and the sun.
You fixed all the boundaries of the earth;
you made both summer and winter.
— *Psalm 74:15-16*◊

Weeks

Pray one of the following, according to the time of day.

Morning:

Early in the morning,
our song shall rise to thee.
— *Holy! Holy! Holy! (Reginald Heber, 1826)*

Midday:

I was glad when they said to me,
"Let us go to the house of the Lord."
— *Psalm 122:1*$^\diamond$

Evening:

Let my prayer be set forth in your sight as incense,
the lifting up of my hands as the evening sacrifice.
— *Psalm 141:2*$^\diamond$

Night:

Guide us waking, O Lord, and guard us sleeping;
that awake we may watch with Christ,
and asleep we may rest in peace.
— *Compline*$^\diamond$

Following the seventh bead:
Glory be to the Father, and to the Son,
and to the Holy Spirit.
As it was in the beginning, is now,
and ever shall be, world without end. Amen.

Dimissory

The grace of our Lord Jesus Christ,
and the love of God,

**and the fellowship of the Holy Spirit,
be with us all evermore. Amen.**
— *2 Corinthians 13:14*[◊]

or

May the God of hope
**fill us with all joy and peace in believing
through the power of the Holy Spirit. Amen.**
— *Romans 15:13*[◊]

In the name of the Father, and of the Son,
and of the Holy Spirit. **Amen.**

About the Author

The Rev'd Dr. William Ingle-Gillis is a jobbing parish priest in the Heart of Monmouthshire Ministry Area in South Wales, and Assistant Director of Vocations for Monmouth Diocese. A Texan raised in Georgia, he moved to the United Kingdom in 1996 to study, and then stayed to be ordained in 2004. All of his parish ministry has happened in South Wales.

Many moons ago, William studied German, then religion, at Baylor University in Waco, Texas; theology at King's College, London; and specifically for the priesthood at Westcott House, Cambridge. For some years, he also taught theology and ethics to the ordinands at St. Michael's College (now St. Padarn's Institute), Llandaff. Previous to joining HoM MA he served parish groups based in Caldicot, Caerwent, Penhow, and Newport.

As a priest in the liberal catholic tradition of Anglicanism, Father William sets a lot of store by the sacraments; the liturgy; spiritual exploration; and, most of all, generosity and goodness towards all who cross our thresholds, regardless of whether they themselves believe in God, regardless of their sexuality, their gender, their past life ... regardless of anything. All are welcome.

Married to the Rev'd Sally Ingle-Gillis, the pair have a large family of two daughters and four sons, two cats, and even a turtle. Personal interests include science fiction; languages (Spanish in particular); barbecue, both Texas and Georgia style (brisket and pulled pork, respectively); computers and gizmos; comedy of the *Futurama* and *Rick & Morty* ilk; music in general and, in particular, the Texas country scene, as well as norteño and tejano. And, once again, cats ... any cats ... all the cats!

Made in the USA
Las Vegas, NV
22 March 2025

19955729R00111